Testimo...

To often, being single breeds negativity from others and the person alike as to why they haven't found a mate. The One by Tonia East gives single readers insight on the purpose of this stage in their lives. Each chapter describes God's love for us, gives insight on personal relationships and how they relate to our relationship with God, how to let go of the pains of our past, and how to pursue God's purpose for our lives. The One is instrumental in helping to reveal who we really are - "The Ones" who walk in God's love throughout our lives.
Tanya Finney, Author - Love Letters: Connecting the heart of man to God

Virtuous best describes her. Tonia East is a woman of great strenghth, unlimited ability, and a wealth of wisdom. In her book, The One, Tonia gives valuable insight into our highest priority in life, seeking first the kingdom of God and His righteousness.
Craig Dennis, Principal Financial Analyst, Coca Cola Company

Your unique experiences, insights and examples and your wonderful spirit, energy and enthusiasm – inspired, informed and encouraged everyone."
Fran Burst-Terranella, Burst Video/Film, Inc.

Tonia East is a demonstration of a true woman of God. Her dedication and love for the things of God has inspired many.The One provokes others to trust God during their time of singleness. I salute Ms. East for her sacrifice in not only writing her new book The One, but living what she writes.
Tracey J. Johnson, Author/Speaker/ CEO of GENESIS KTISIS Inc.

Jariah & Arieyanne,
Continue to allow to
lead & guide your path.
Louia Ew
Deut. 31:8

The One

A Womans Search for
Eternal Love

The One

A Womans Search for
Eternal Love

By: TONIA EAST

Higher Heights Publishing
Atlanta, GA

Unless otherwise indicated, all Scripture quotations are taken from the New King James Version of the Bible.

All Scripture quotations marked NIV are taken from the New International Version of the Bible.

All Scripture quotations marked NLT are taken from the New Living Translation Version of the Bible.

All Scripture quotations marked KJV are taken from the King James Version of the Bible.

THE ONE
ISBN 978-0-578-01087-8
Copyright © 2009 by Tonia East

Higher Heights Publishing
Atlanta, Georgia

Dedication Page

I dedicate this book to my mother, Ruth East, who has shown me by her example how to live as a virtuous woman and is responsible for introducing me to THE ONE.

Acknowledgments

Where would I be without the support of so many amazing people? I am truly grateful to all of the phenomenal men and women who shared invaluable advice in this book. I know I am a better woman because of your words of wisdom. Special thanks to Dr. Wanda Davis-Turner, Dr. Gloria Morrow, Min. Jaquatte Williams, and Valorie Burton for your contributions. Thanks to my writers' group, Tanya, Claudette, and Kim, for your accountability in completing this project. Thank you to my mother for your continuous support of the vision of God for my life. Thank you to my spiritual parents Bishop Eddie Long and to First Lady Vanessa Long, for modeling grace and elegance in your everyday life. I am forever grateful to Ms. Betty Chaney for editing my last book, Changing Lanes, and this book. Thank you so much to Higher Heights Publishing, for taking my words and creating an artistic masterpiece in the cover and design of the book. Thank you to Sara and everyone at Bethany International for your assistance in publication. Last, but certainly not least, I must thank the lover of my soul, my confidant, my savior, the inspiration for this book, THE ONE and only living God.

Contents

Foreword

By Dr. Wanda Davis-Turner

Last February, on a cold, wet, dreary evening – in fact Valentine's night, I sat in my bedroom "alone". "Alone"- but hoping. "Alone" – but wishing. "Alone" – but dreaming! Hoping, wishing, dreaming about what? An opportunity to share a wonderful meal with a wonderful man – on a wonderful night. But how could I? I am single and a woman. How could I? I am single and shy. How could I … I am single and frightened of new relationships. Suddenly, the voice of God whispered to my hurting heart… 'want to go to dinner?' "Yes, Lord", I replied. Then put on your best and take yourself! Take myself? … I thought! The restaurant will be full of couples…smiling, holding hands and looking into one another's eyes. And who will be with me? "I will," answered Jesus. Put on your beautiful mink coat, mink hat… and new boots. Get in your own car and drive your own self to that wonderful new restaurant, Landon's on Cascade in Atlanta. I did just that!

Wow…what a powerful wake up call. That the season I entered as a single woman almost seven years ago… was not just about Wanda. But even more so, it was about "Wanda and the One"…. my journey as a whole, complete person. Alone but not lonely for how could I be alone and yet walk with the Creator, the Redeemer, the Healer, the Provider… THE ONE! Who from the beginning of time empowered and created me just like himself!

It is exciting to begin chronicling my journey as a single woman and bump "intentionally" into Tonia N. East, who like me is assigned to empower single women to seek, more than anything else in life, THE ONE, which is Christ Jesus. Because the Word of the Lord declares, "seek and ye shall find, knock and the door shall be opened"-we each have the wonderful challenging experience of seeking and knocking that our lives might be enriched and blessed so that we can enrich and bless others. Tonia has tackled this journey so masterfully. So many women have struggled through the years to find love, provision, direction, peace and passion…but have walked past the very "love, provision, direction, peace, and passion" they seek – which is housed only in Christ Jesus.

Wanda, is there anything wrong with longing, hoping, and desiring for a Godly relationship with a Godly man…No! But before reaching out to find that relationship with a Godly man, we need to find the God of that Godly man! All too often we as singles focus on the text "he that finds a wife, finds a good thing and obtains favor of the Lord" – not realizing that in Psalms 65:4, we are encouraged to note, "Blessed is the man You choose, and cause to approach You. That he may dwell in Your court…We shall be satisfied with the goodness…" (NKJ) Rightfully so, the man is to "find a wife" but note, according to David, we as single women do not have to choose every man that finds us! We can make quality decisions to choose only what God desires for us…peace, joy, hope, and faith. We can make quality decisions to choose only who God desires for us… not "men of God" but "Godly men." There is a great difference.

Tonia's work literally takes you on a journey to wholeness, to perfection, to joy… and the destination is victory! If you are not ready to mature and grow; if you are not ready to take responsibility for your life as a strong, vibrant, necessary woman in the Kingdom of God; then put this book down right now! But, if you are in real search of eternal love and lifelong joy, then keep reading, for Tonia has found the answers you desire. You will find such delight, peace and hope… that when "the man" approaches you, you almost ignore him for fear he will interrupt your journey of love and hope found only in your relationship with Jesus the Christ.

Introduction

Do you remember being a little girl and dreaming about your wedding day, picturing your beautiful white wedding dress, smelling the lovely flowers that decorate the church? Seeing the pews filled with adoring friends and family, hearing the organ playing the wedding march, and seeing all of your very best friends as you saunter down the aisle. As you approach the altar, you meet your handsome husband, dressed in his tuxedo, and saying the words that will change your life forever, "I do". And then, from that day forward, you imagined the rest of your life as being picture perfect.

As children, you played house with friends, and of course you always wanted to be the wife, married to the successful husband. The songs and movies that fill the airways and draw people to the theater continually perpetuate all of these romantic fantasies. From the time we are little girls, we are constantly inundated with media images of the perfect relationship. Many of the images we see are not based on realistic relationships and give the perception that once you find "the one," everything in life is perfect. Even our friends, family, and strangers are asking one question, "Have you found the one?" Almost every popular TV drama centers on one or more characters in pursuit of "the one." Every magazine is obsessed with the relationships of popular entertainers and musicians. Even if you are not one for daydreaming and don't really watch TV or read magazines, you might be driving down the highway minding your own business and a billboard may ask, "Are you single? Are you looking for the one?" Web sites grossing billions of dollars are there to help you in your search for "the one." Once you reach your mid to late twenties, family, friends, and people you don't even know, make it their personal mission to help you in the quest for "the one."

I have had the honor of being in many of my friends' weddings and it's inevitable that the question will rear its head. "So when are you planning on getting married?" Usually my response is, "Your guess is as good as mine." Believe me when I do find the one, everyone will know, but until then I am not obsessed with wondering when that time will be.

However, this wasn't always the case. I remember having it all planned out to the exact day I would be walking down the aisle. Then, that day comes and goes; the person you just knew was "the one," turns out to be just another one. Feelings of shame, depression, guilt, and loneliness begin to take root. You begin to wonder if the day you dreamed about as a little girl was just a fantasy and not a reality. So often, a single woman feels that something must be wrong with her if she is not in a relationship at every moment in life. Surely, singleness is a disease that must be cured. People will spend all their money, time, and energy to rid themselves of this terrible disease. Then, I began to see that while we are worried about this one area of our lives, a greater, much more damaging tragedy was occurring. Our dreams and goals were being neglected and forgotten while all of our attention was directed toward finding "the one." In college, I remember seeing my friends flunking classes and completely giving up on life after a dramatic break-up. After college, I began seeing young women that I admired for their love of life, academic excellence, and grand ambitions fall into relationships that stifled their creativity and did not allow them to become all that God had ordained for their lives.

I spoke at length to a group of single women that shared some of these same concerns. Their thoughts are shared throughout the book. One thing they all agreed upon was that their singleness has been a time for understanding who they are and who God has called them to be. It's also a time to become prepared for all the different roles women play in life. We are learning to be better friends, sisters, mothers, wives, teachers, and students in all areas of life. One woman commented on how sometimes we allow ourselves to be defined by our singleness, but there are so many aspects that make up who we are and we have to position ourselves to be used by God in various roles.

I look back at my teenage years and wonder how much farther I would be in my spiritual journey had I spent less time consumed with "the one" and more time seeking The ONE. We cannot change the past, but we can redirect our future. We can save our money and redirect our time. There is no need to waste precious energy chasing after everyone that could potentially be "the one." Realize it is not necessarily that something is wrong with you. And guess what, you are okay with God. In fact, you are more than okay; you are fearfully and wonderfully made by Him.

Actually, now is the time when He has you all to Himself. After reading this book, I pray you will realize as I did, that singleness is not something that we should regret, but it is one of the only times in our lives that we can focus solely on who God has called us to be. Paul, one of the Bible's most prolific authors states, "But I want you to be without care. He who is unmarried cares for the things of the Lord. But he who is married cares about the things of the world – how he may please his wife."[1] So what a tragedy it is if we are always stressed about pleasing others and never have a time in our lives which we can devote to pleasing God and becoming the best person we can be.

One thing we must realize is that this is a time in our lives when God is shaping us and molding us to receive all that He has in store for our future. It's unfortunate that many people young and old find themselves in relationships and then find they are "growing apart." Many times it's not that they grew apart, but that they were never truly going in the same direction. But, how are we to know what direction our lives are going in if we never spend time seeking The ONE? He tells us,

For I know the thoughts that I think toward you, says the Lord, thoughts of peace and not evil, to give you a future and a hope. Then you will call upon Me, and I will listen to you. And you will

seek Me and find Me when you search for Me with all your heart.[2]

God's thoughts are to give us a hope and a future. It is not His will for us to end up hurt or divorced just a few short years after we marry. There are more divorces at earlier ages than ever before. In order to search for God with all our heart, He has to take first place in our affection and devotion. When we seek and find The One, He will lead us to the people that will help us to complete His will for our lives, including "the one." Now doesn't that take away the stress of having to always be constantly on the lookout for Mr. Right? Knowing some of the choices I have made in the past, I would much rather put my destiny in the hands of One who is all-knowing and has my very best interests at heart. Though I am sure my family and friends want the best for me, only God knows His ultimate plan for my life and the person who is uniquely ordained to fit that plan. When we know who we are, we can more accurately know who we need. When we seek "the one" without finding The ONE, there can be devastating consequences. Whether it is your desire to be married or to just live a life that is more fully devoted to God's will , my prayer is that God will reveal the awesomeness of His plans for you as you continue to read through each chapter.

For if by one man's offense death reigned through the one, much more those who receive abundance of grace and of the gift of righteousness will reign in life through the One, Jesus Christ.[3]

Chapter One
Greater Love: Know Greater Love

*As a child of God, divinely created to glorify Him, a woman's primary
relationship is her relationship with God. You can get by without anything
else, but a relationship with the Father is essential.*
Bishop Eddie L . Long

Lonely Lauri

Lauri wonders what to buy for a woman that has every-thing. She can't believe Victoria will be married in three days. She begins to wonder if her dreams of romance will ever be realized. She doesn't want to appear sad when all of the girls get together tonight to celebrate Victoria's last days as a single woman. But she just can't help thinking about the fact that she too should be celebrating her last days of singleness. She can't believe that Troy called it off. After the invitations were sent out, the church had been booked; her bride's maids had been chosen. Now she felt so ashamed, so unworthy, and so angry. She put up a good front, but the hurt was beginning to turn into bitterness and she prayed it didn't become rage. It was just a lot to handle. Victoria and Lauri were planning their weddings together and now she was alone.

"How could he do this to me?"

To think that she was always the one that had broken up with all of her past boyfriends. She was known as, Lauri the love and leave 'em girl. Was this some sort of sick karma? She just never wanted to be the one who was left and now on the most important day of her life, she was being left out to dry. She finally found someone that she thought she could open up to and let down her guard. Troy proved to be worse than all the others. He probably knew I would leave him too, if he hadn't proposed. The funny thing is that he was probably right.

If Lauri only knew how much love her first love, had for her, she would then be able to see that God had never left her alone. Lauri felt as if every man she had ever loved had abandoned her, including her own father, which was probably why she was so quick to end every relationship. At least, then she felt that she had control. Regardless of how many guys had taken her attention away from her first love, He was always right there, sending gentle reminders of how much He loved her. Many of us seem to overlook the love of our Lord, until we feel that others have forsaken or abandoned us. Unlike people who pull away from intimacy, He promises that if we draw close to Him, He will draw closer to us. We can never love Him too much or be able to comprehend the depth of His love for us.[4] We must understand that He will never be abandon or forsake us.

How precious are your thoughts to me, O God! How great is the sum of them! If I could count them, they would be more in number than the sand; When I wake, I am still with You.[5]

Busy Brittany
Lauri didn't have much time before she would have to meet Brittany on the other side of the mall. She knew she

would be upset if she were even a minute late. Brittany was always rushing from one thing to the next, without a moment to spare. Between her own daily beauty regimens, her high-paced job as a corporate executive, and her various roles at church and in other organizations, she had no time to waste. Though she has accomplished many things, she still feels unfulfilled. It's more than just the loneliness that comes from being recently divorced; even when she was married there was a void that her husband Josh could never fill. She knows that something is still missing, but she isn't exactly sure what it is. She is far too busy to take time to think about it. This is the only life she knows.

From the time she was a child, her mother had her in every activity at school or church so that she wouldn't have known what to do with herself if she had to actually slow down for a minute. The apple doesn't fall far from the tree; though her mother was a stay-at-home mom, she worked harder than anyone she knew. She was president of the Parent Teacher Board, had her own baking business on the side, and was the church choir director and Sunday school teacher. Her father worked late hours and even some weekends. He always tried to make it to her special events, but even if he didn't, Brittany knew he cared. After college, Brittany began working just as hard herself and has adopted her father's corporate savvy and her mother's community involvement. As busy as she is there are still times when she feels as if there is something more that God has called her to do.

Perhaps you share Brittany's feelings of longing for something more. I remember when I first graduated from my Master's program, I had been so consumed with school that I didn't know what to do with myself. However, it was during that time that God began to reveal His will for my life. I knew there was something more, but I had to slow down a minute to hear what God was calling me to do. It was during that time that I wrote my first book. Though it was one of the best times, it was also difficult for me to learn to trust God to provide for me. I couldn't find a job for months after graduating and it seemed like so many doors were closing, but at the same time God was opening doors for me to go to Europe, to spend more time with Him, and to enjoy fellowship with my family and friends. Our society is so consumed with activity, and event after event, that we can miss God altogether. We should never be too busy, to pray, to rest, to enjoy each day. If we are too busy when we are single, it will only get worse when we get married. Now is the time to seek God for His plan and purpose for our lives.

Are we more like Martha or Mary? Busy Brittany is definitely more like Martha. Jesus had just come into town and Martha being the gracious hostess welcomed Him into her home. While Martha was busy cleaning the house and doing all the things she felt "needed" to be done, Mary was sitting at the feet of Jesus and heard His word. I know how my mother is about bringing company into an untidy house and I may have shared Martha's concern. I am sure Martha felt justified in doing what she thought was a good thing, but Mary was doing a God thing. We must be willing to put our agendas aside to sit at the feet of our Master. Brittany is longing for a word, but like Martha she is too busy to hear Him. Jesus told Martha,

Martha, Martha you are worried and troubled about many things. But one thing is needed, and Mary has chosen that good part, which will not be taken from her.[6]

THE ONE

Though we feel there are so many things we need to do, the time we spend time with The One is most important. There was an illustration I once saw in Bible study that showed how we must do first things first. We say we want to spend more time with God, but by the end of the day we're exhausted. They took a glass jar and showed how this is our life and they took some large stones to show the major things like God, family, ministry, etc. Then they had a bag of little stones to show all the little errands we have to do like cleaning, feeding the dog, grocery shopping. When you put all the little stones in first, there is never enough room for the most important things in life, but if you put first things first all the other little stones will fill in the empty spaces. If a few errands don't get done, it is not like missing out on time with God. So let's make the most of the time that we have to spend with God, our family, and even to do the things that you enjoy doing. It seems crazy to be single and not have time for you, but it's very possible. Schedule some time in your day to take care of you and do things that make you feel special. Remember if you don't think you're special, why would anyone else.

Hesitant Heather

Heather is the one Lauri and Brittany come to when they need some sound advice. It seems as if Heather always has a well-thought out answer, weighing all the pros and cons. The unfortunate thing is that Heather is so hesitant about making a decision, she often lets opportunities pass her by. Heather remembers watching the movie, The Last Holiday, and feeling like Georgia before she found out about her fatal condition. There were so many aspirations she had and things she wanted to do, but would it take a life and death emergency to shake her out of her comfort zone.

She longed to start her own travel agency. She had researched the industry and knew all about the business. In her spare time she would cut out pictures of exotic places she longed to visit. The reality was she didn't even have a passport. Her last major trip was to Birmingham, Alabama, for her great aunt's funeral and that was only a three-hour drive away.

Life for Heather was common and predictable. Heather went from work to church, an occasional visit with friends, and back to square one. She didn't feel challenged or satisfied with her current job, but she did earn a decent living as an accountant. She knew she was ready for a change, but was afraid to leave the comforts of her pre-dictable life. Yes, it was monotonous and boring, but at least she knew what to expect. If she ventured out to start her own business, what would she do if she failed? What if she couldn't pay her bills? What if people no longer respected her decisions as wise and well thought out? She prayed to God for the courage to overcome her fears.

What Heather didn't know is that God had answered her prayer, but it was up to her to believe His word. God loves us so much that He sent His Son that we would not just have life, but that we may have it "more abundantly."[7] Different versions of the text read that we "might have" or "may have" abundant life; either way it's not automatic. We have to make a decision to live our best life, every day. We can settle for the comforts of mediocrity or we can make a choice to live each day to the fullest. We have to know that when we take time to spend with The One to know our purpose and what we are called to do, we have to trust that He will not lead us astray. We can be like Hesitant Heather and focus on all the "what if's" or we can focus on what we know. If we know that God is truly our provider and not our job, if we know that the steps of the righteous are ordered by the Lord, if we know that He has not given us a spirit of fear, but of power, love, and a sound mind, if we know that we should not be anxious about anything, and if we are confident that it is God that will complete the work He has begun in us, then what are we waiting for? Yes, we must count the cost and have a plan in place, but we have to actually believe that it is possible. What if Bill Gates was afraid to step out of the box and do something that had never been done before, not only would he be affected the entire world would be at a loss. We have to realize that we too have a gift that is not just to be a blessing to our lives, but a blessing to others. The longer we wait the more people miss out on the blessing God has placed inside of us. The one thing we should fear is not what would happen if we failed in trying, but what would happen if we didn't complete the work we were given to do. One of my favorite quotes reads,

Our deepest fear is not that we are inadequate. Our deepest fear is that we are powerful beyond measure. It is our light, not our darkness that most frightens us. We ask ourselves who am I to be brilliant, gorgeous, talented, fabulous? Actually, who are you not to be? You are a child of God. Your playing small does not serve the world.[8]

We have to learn to see ourselves the way God sees us --in His image, fearfully and wonderfully made. We were not an accident or a surprise to God. Before we were even in our mother's womb, He had called us to a special purpose. He told Jeremiah that before I formed you in your mother's womb He had already ordained him to be a prophet to the nations.[9] Yet, Jeremiah gave the excuse that he was too young and inexperienced. God encouraged him not to be afraid of what people may do, when he was already given power to overcome nations. Just as He called Jeremiah to a specific role, He knew there was a role we would have to play on this earth. He placed in us everything we need to succeed in that role. We can wait behind the scenes and complain that we are too young, too old, too inexperienced, too broke, or we can take the part He has given us to play and know that He has already given us everything we need to succeed.

I sought the Lord, and He heard me and delivered me
from all my fears.[10]

Careless Carrie

Now, Carrie and Heather were exact opposites. When Lauri and Brittany wanted to do something wild and crazy, like bungee jumping or an impromptu road trip, Carrie was the first person they called. They knew that Carrie would always be ready for a good time. Heather could live vicariously through Carrie, but was often embarrassed by her public scenes and wild behavior. Carrie always had condescending eyes watching her every behavior. Growing up as a PK (preacher's kid)didn't help. She had once tried to do everything perfectly, but it never seemed like it was quite good enough. She was an amazing singer and people would always praise her for her unique vocal ability, but it seemed that this talent was the only thing she was praised for as a child.

Once Carrie left the strict confines of her small town to go to college, she finally felt like she was free. Everything she was told not to do, she did. By her sophomore year she had dropped out of college to pursue her singing career and had moved to Los Angeles with her boyfriend, John, who was an aspiring actor. She was a waitress by day and singer by night. Carrie sang at nightclubs, birthday parties, weddings, but it was rare that she found herself in the one place where she had first learned to sing, the church. Carrie may have been many things, but she was real and she didn't want to feel like a hypocrite. She would occasionally go to church when she was feeling especially down. Her boyfriend John found it hard to get consistent acting gigs and often took out his frustration on her. She knew he loved her it was just hard times. She didn't have any family and very few friends who John would allow her to see, so she often felt that there was nowhere to go, if she ever did leave him. No matter how bad the fighting, beating, or emotional abuse was the night before, John always made it up the next day. He would prepare a romantic dinner and apologize for everything. She knew that no matter what happened he was the one. He was the first boy she gave her heart to and knew he would be the last. When Carrie found out she was pregnant, though she was scared she was excited to be having John's child. However, when she told John, he didn't share her enthusiasm. He insisted that she must be pregnant with someone else's child, because he knew he was not the father. He had too much to lose, his career and his plans. Carrie insisted that there was no one else, but that didn't stop him from giving her one of the worse beatings he had ever given her. It was as if he wanted to beat the child out of her. Everything went black; the next thing she remembered was waking up in the hospital and seeing her parents praying at her bedside. Her only friend, Sasha, had found her that night in a pool of her own blood and called the ambulance and her parents. John had packed his things and left Carrie for dead. It was a week before she came out of the coma. Miraculously, her baby survived and nine months later her daughter Selah was born. She returned to Georgia to be near her family. She knew she had been careless in the past but she made a decision that with God's help she was going to be a good mother.

She still loved having a good time, but she did take her role as a mother seriously. Carrie was more than an occasional visitor at her parent's church, and decided to sing in the choir again. She went back to school and finished her degree in business, but wasn't exactly sure how she would use it. She often changed jobs; it just seemed like none of her job choices fit who she was or who she wanted to be. She knew that more than ever she needed to seek God's direction for her life. Though she may not have always made the right choices before, when she woke up from that coma, she knew that God had given another chance to live and she didn't want to waste it wandering aimlessly.

We, like Carrie, have all made mistakes and fallen short, but it's up to us to seek The One in order to make better decisions for our future. Regardless of what we may have done, He is more than willing to forgive us and give us another chance to live the life we were purposed to live in Him. We can all ask where we would be without the grace of God in our lives. Many of us would not even be here today, if it wasn't for His grace. Whether past relationships have left us emotionally or financially bankrupt, our Father is able to restore and renew us with His love. He assures us that there is now no condemnation in Christ Jesus. If our Heavenly Father does not condemn us we shouldn't allow others to do so, and we must not condemn ourselves. Often times, we were doing the best we knew to do at the time. God has never left us and is standing with open arms, ready to receive us into His loving bosom. He is at the door knocking, but it is up to us to let Him in. We often make time to talk with everyone except Him and He is the only one who can meet our every need. When we are at our lowest, He shows Himself strongest in our life.

Desperate Debra

The women laughed at how they used to be boy crazy in high school. However, it seemed that Debra, never out grew this stage. Finding "the one" was a full time job for Debra; you never know when he might show up. He could be at the grocery store, her job, her church, the club, or even driving next to her on the highway. No matter where she was, she would not hesitate to give a fine young man her full attention. No, Debra did not believe in being subtle. If she wanted someone's attention, she was surely going to get it, one way or another. Perhaps growing up as a middle child of eight children and two busy parents, left her starving for attention at an early age, but the attention she got from her Uncle, left her feeling dirty and ashamed. He was shot in a drug deal that went bad and she never told her parents about the years of molestation she endured. By the time she went to high school her coke bottle shape had all the boys' attention and she loved every minute of it. She didn't realize that she was giving a little piece of herself to every guy she was with, but she began to feel as if she really wasn't worth anything anymore. When she went off to college, she desperately wanted to make something of herself. She met Lauri and Carrie her first semester of college. They had some wild times together, but they all have settled down over the years. Now that they are in their thirties or just shy of thirty, they had families and careers to worry about. Debra, married twice before, felt like her biological clock was ticking louder than ever. She had three abortions when she was just a teenager, but now was ready to be married and start a family. She was willing to do whatever it took to find the man of her dreams.

The sad thing was Debra never realized He was right there. The only perfect and unconditional love is from God. He so wanted to heal all the places where men had hurt her and show her true love. Debra would never be able to receive true love if she didn't begin to love herself. Regardless of how others may have labeled her, there is a God that still loves her like the Samaritan woman at the well, who was shocked that Jesus would ask her for a drink since Jews typically did not speak to Samaritans, who were seen as unclean, God loves Debra. Jesus had responded to the Samaritan woman by saying, "if you knew the gift of God" and who I truly am, you would know that I would have given you living water[11]. Jesus knew that she was thirsting for more than a physical refreshing, her spirit needed to be refreshed and though she had had five husbands and was currently living with someone else, only He could quench that thirst. Jesus didn't condemn her. He merely states how this is the hour when she must learn to worship the Father in spirit and in truth. Debra, like the woman at the well, had to be able to let go of the past and seek God with her whole heart. God desires that we give Him our all. The Word tells us the Lord our God, the Lord is One, or also translated as the only One.[12] There is none beside Him and there is one thing that He requires from us.

You shall love the Lord your God with all your heart, with all your soul, and with all your strength.[13]

The beautiful thing is when we love God and see ourselves in God, we can love ourselves and others unconditionally.

Too Through Tina

Everyone knows the last thing Tina wants to discuss is a man. She is too tired, too distrusting, and too through with the men in her life. She has made up her mind that the last thing she wants to do is be married again. Been there, done that, could write a book about it. She married Tyrone, right out of high school. She thought nothing could be worse than the rules and constraints her mother and father had put on her. Oh, how wrong she was. Tyrone had more rules than her parents ever did. He wouldn't allow her to hangout with her friends, even though he could stay out all hours of the night and come meandering in the next morning. She could barely call her own family. When she had her first child, Sarah, she thought things would be better and they were at first. Then after having Tyrone Jr., instead of being intensely jealous of other men, he became jealous of his own children. He accused her of never having time for him anymore, when actually he was working later and later. When he wasn't working he was staying out all night drinking with his friends. Tina tried to do everything she could to show him that she loved him. She would prepare elaborate dinners and plan time for them to go out alone, but her plans were always ruined when he had to work late or do overtime on the weekends.

Tina remembered how they used to spend every moment together in high school and when they weren't together they were on the phone. After they were married, everything changed. It was as if she were living with a stranger. They rarely ever talked and hardly even touched. She began to wonder if Tyrone was cheating on her. Tina began to find numbers of women he claimed were business associates. One day when he was away on a weekend trip, Sarah became extremely ill. When she called his business partner, he was surprised to learn that she was not on the trip with him. He had booked the flight for both of them. When she called his room and another woman answered the phone, all suspicion was removed. As bad as things were, she had never thought he was truly unfaithful. After that incident, she lost faith in everything, in men, in herself, and in God. How could God allow this to happen to her? She found it difficult to even pray anymore, what was the point. Everything she had prayed for had come crumbling down and there was no way the pieces could be put back together again.

She moved back in with her parents until she could find a decent job, which was no easy task for a woman who hadn't worked in ten years. She went back to school and is now becoming a paralegal. Tyrone does provide child support, but she would just as soon have him out of her life all together. Tina tried to stay supportive of her children's relationship with their father, but it was difficult. He had remarried and gone on with his life and here she was struggling to make ends meet. Yes, Tina was too through with all men. Men who were not put off by her sour disposition and attempted to approach her, soon found out that she was uninterested, unavailable, and unimpressed. She would rather get a root canal with no anesthesia than to so much as think about another relationship with any man. She lived by the Tina Turner song, What's Love got to Do With It. Everything. God's love has everything to do with it.

Regardless of what people have done, when we seek The One, He is able to give us the strength to forgive. As long as Tina holds onto her anger against Tyrone, the longer it will take for her wounds to heal. Her bitterness against all men prevents her from being able to trust any man. Her unforgiveness may lead her looking for love in all the wrong places. I have seen young women turn to a life of homosexuality because of the pain men have caused in their lives. Though they desire a relationship with the Lord their unforgiveness creates a wall of pain that only God can heal, if they would let Him. Tina is literally hurting herself. Bless God that He is not as unforgiving as His children. Time after time He forgives us and allows us to begin again. Grace, is God's unmerited favor, meaning that it isn't because we deserve it, but because of the blood of Christ that was shed for remission of our sins. We could never do enough to earn the grace of God. Grace is a gift. In order for us to receive the forgiveness of God, we must also offer forgiveness to others. When Jesus taught his disciples to pray He instructs them not to pray for your needs for God already knows what you need before you even ask. However when we pray we should pray in this manner,

Our Father in heaven, Hallowed be Your name,
Your kingdom come. Your will be done on earth as it is in heaven.
Give us this day our daily bread.
And forgive us our debts, As we forgive our debtors.[14]

Virtuous Victoria

All the girls were coming to celebrate Victoria's wedding. Victoria has had her share of ups and downs, but now it was her time to celebrate. She had been in both of Debra's weddings, as well as Brittany's and wondered when her time would come. She was actively involved in her church and worked as a social worker. She truly enjoyed being able to re-unite families. She understood what it was like to be separated from loved ones at an early age. Her mother had left her with her grandmother when she was only three years old, too consumed with her desire to live the fast life of drugs, alcohol, and more men then she could count.

In hindsight, she can see how the hand of God was on her life, even though she felt abandoned. Her Nanna was the most amazing and kind woman she knew. Nanna always had people over to enjoy her good home-cooking. Everyone knew if they came to Nanna's house, especially on Sunday, there would be a hot meal waiting. Nanna never turned anyone away and somehow there was always enough food. Victoria learned how to trust God to provide by watching her Nana continuously give to others. Her grandfather had passed away before she was born and she learned how to trust God to care for her. Nanna was well cared for, with her beautiful Sunday suits, accompanied by matching hat and purse ensemble. She would always say, "This old thing, well you know God's a keeper" and smile with her beautiful, contagious grin. Yes, she would not be the woman she was today if it were not for her Nanna.

It took a long time but she was finally able to for-give her parents for what they had done to her. For years she felt that she was to blame, but Nanna, would tell her over and over that it wasn't her fault. One day, she finally believed it and knew that God knew her Nanna was the one that needed to raise her. She was a little strict, but there is no telling what would have happened to her if she had stayed with her mother. Her mother eventually overdosed, when she was in high school. Victoria remembers going to the funeral and being overcome with so many emotions of sadness and anger she eventually became numb. She wished she had her parents to see her graduate from high school and college with honors, but she thanked God for Nanna.

She remembers how nervous she was to introduce Nanna to Kevin as her boyfriend and soon after fiancé. They had known Kevin from church, but Victoria never thought they would ever be together. Kevin wasn't really her type, or so she thought. Kevin began to make subtle hints that he was interested in Victoria as more than a friend, but Victoria just didn't see him as the one. One day, she thought about all the things she wanted in a husband and realized that Kevin possessed almost every quality. He was giving, kind, intelligent, successful, and most importantly truly had a heart to serve God. She remembered praying to God to show her if Kevin was the one that He had ordained for her life. She always thought she would eventually marry her high school sweetheart Michael. Kevin was cute, but Michael was fine. The only problem was that Michael knew he was fine and so did all the ladies. She never really felt like she could fully trust him. Just when she was beginning to let Kevin in, Michael calls her up out of the blue to tell her how much he misses her. She was overcome with all the emotions of the past and prayed to God for direction. She remembers opening her Bible and reading,

Do not look at his appearance or at his physical stature, because I have refused Him. For the Lord does not see as man sees; for man looks at the outward appearance, but the Lord looks at the heart.[15]

She knew then that Michael was just a counterfeit. Kevin was the one that would truly love her with the love of Christ. Kevin was the one that had sought the heart of God and truly represented all the qualities she would want in a husband.

God rewards those that diligently seek after Him. Victoria learned that only God could reveal the man he had ordained for her. So, if it is your desire to marry, God will give you, your husband or wife. Sounds too good to be true? Just look at the godly connection made for Abraham's son, Isaac. Isaac was busy serving his father, when Abraham sent his servant to find a wife for Isaac. Abraham's servant was given very specific directions not to choose a wife from the Canaanites, but to choose one from his own country and lineage. Even then it was important to be equally yoked. Abraham's servant was afraid of what would happen if he chose a woman who did not want to come back with him: Which is a perfectly understandable concern, considering she would have to leave her family and everything familiar to her, to be married to someone she had never met. Abraham assured him that God would send His angels before him. Abraham's servant did not take this assignment lightly, but first sought God for direction and favor. He prayed,

O Lord God of my master Abraham, please give me
success this day, and show kindness to my master
Abraham. ...Now let it be that the young woman to whom
I say 'Please letdown your pitcher that I may drink,' and
she says, 'Drink, and I will also give your camels a drink'
– let her be the one You have appointed for Your servant
Isaac.[16]

THE ONE

Lo and behold before Abraham's servant could finish his prayer, here comes Rebekah strolling down to the well with her pitcher on her shoulder. Not only was Rebekah beautiful outwardly, she radiated an inward godly beauty. Abraham's servant ran to meet her and sure enough she gladly gave him a drink as well as offered to water his camels. Rebekah stated, "I will draw water for your camels until they have finished drinking." Now this was no small task, considering he traveled with ten of his master's camels that could all drink a considerable amount of water. They may have not finished drinking for quite a while considering the fact that camels are able to survive long journeys by storing water in their humps. It wasn't until after all the camels had finished drinking that Abraham's servant was convinced that Rebekah was the one. Then he endowed her with gifts of gold and found that she was actually from Abraham's own country and lineage. Is God not faithful to those who seek His will. As Rebekah gladly served the Lord by serving him, all her needs were met. Just like Victoria and Rebekah we must decide to wait on God to reveal His perfect plan for our lives.

Prayer

Lord, thank you for your unconditional love towards me. Thank you for never leaving me or forsaking me. Regardless of what I may have experienced in past relationships, I will put my trust in You. Lord you are The One I can give my whole heart with abandon. Forgive me for the times I have placed other things before you. You are The One that has kept me throughout the years. You will continue to keep me in your loving arms, safe from all harm. Thank you for being my shield and protection. Thank you for being the lover of my soul. Only you can remove the hurt, the pain, and the fear. Your perfect love casts out all fear. You have not given me a spirit of fear, but of power, love, and a sound mind. Bless your name, for you alone are worthy of praise.

Chapter Two
Our Provider

Busy Brittany is so busy rushing from here to there that she never took time to seek God's will for her day. We should never be too busy to spend time with God. It's so important to take time each day just to acknowledge His presence in our lives and listen to what He has to share with us. You wouldn't want to be in a marriage with someone who never even acknowledged your presence or listened to a word you had to say, but told everyone about his deep and abiding love for you. If we are too busy for God in our singleness, it's not going to get any better in marriage. Time with God must take precedence on our To-Do list. I know it does feel difficult at times, but I can attest that the days that I haven't sought His will were least productive. As we spend time with Him, He guides our path in wisdom, protection, and in the way that would allow us to prosper. You never know what accident He has prevented or opportunity He opened up by being in the right place at the right time.

THE ONE

It is good and proper to love our spouses and children, to spend time with them, and to do things for them. The worst error we can commit, however, is to make them idols by putting them ahead of God in our priority list. Seek God first; then bless your spouse, your children, and your friends.[17]

Taking the Lead Role

We have to be careful not to think that we have to take the lead role in our life. I would rather be God's best supporting actress than take the lead any day. We must learn to submit and humble ourselves so that God can shine through us. God exalts the humble and we must realize that our ultimate purpose is to bring about God's will for our lives. Paul warns that we should not seek success out of selfish ambition or conceit, but we should consider others even before ourselves.[18] If Christ even humbled Himself in order to fulfill His Father's will, will we not be required to submit to our Father.

And being found in appearance as a man, He humbled Himself and became obedient to the point of death, even death on the cross. Therefore God also has highly exalted Him and given Him the name above every name.[19]

Just as He promised Abraham, God wants to make our name great, but we must be willing to sacrifice our agendas and die to our will in order for God's will to prevail in our lives. What if God asks you to move immediately and separate yourself from family and friends? Would you be able to reconsider your plans? Abraham had to be willing to leave his family and friends and not even know where God was sending him. God told Abram to go, "To a land I will show you", but He promised that He would make Him a great nation, make his name great, and allow him to be a blessing.[20] We all would be excited about the blessing, but would we be able to make the sacrifice. Sometimes we don't realize how much we may be relying on family or love ones until they are gone. When my father passed away when I was young, I saw how my mother trusted in God and would declare the Word, that she has never seen the righteous forsaken, nor their seed begging bread.[21] Though it was tight, we never went without our needs being met. There may have been some wants we didn't have, but our need was well provided. God promises to meet all our need according to His riches and glory.[22]

I know when God assigned me to leave California to move to Georgia, where I had no family, friends, or even associates, I prayed for confirmation that it was really His will. We have to activate our faith and step out and see God's provision. He didn't promise that it would be easy, but we must obey. When I would step out, He opened a door and I would see His hand of favor preparing the way. It was definitely a sacrifice financially and emotionally, but I grew so much spiritually. It's so important that we take the time to seek Him in prayer and through His word to even know what God is calling us to do. Since I have been in Georgia, God has sent me family and friends who I would have never expected to be in Georgia. God promises that anything we leave, brothers or sisters, mothers or fathers, or property for His sake will be restored to us a hundredfold.[23]

I remember another critical time when I was in college and my roommates and I were looking for a place to stay for the upcoming school year. We had less than a month before we were required to start our summer positions as orientation guides and I remember one of my mother's dear friends and prayer partners telling me to just start packing. I knew she was a woman of faith and I followed her instructions. We were able to find a beautiful town home near campus that was in our budget. We learned to trust God to provide even when we did not understand all the details. If we knew, everything, it would not require faith. As we prepare in faith for the provision, God honors our obedience and exceeds our expectations. We must realize that our thoughts are not His thoughts, for His thoughts are so much higher than our thoughts and His ways are so much higher than our ways.[24] Every word that He has spoken over our lives will be accomplished even if we don't understand how it will take place.

What a privilege it is to even be given the opportunity to reflect the light of God to others, to be able to play even a small role in fulfilling His will in the earth. Regardless of the temporary sacrifice, it will not compare to the glory that will be revealed in us. I remember hearing Jennifer Hudson share her testimony. She stated how she knew she was called to sing, but doors were not opening immediately, in fact many were closing. She auditioned to play a supporting role in Dream Girls, not realizing that it would catapult her career and earn her an academy award for Best Supporting Actress. Several well-known actors are most known for the supporting roles they played more so than the lead roles. We think we are taking a step down and God is actually exalting us to a higher place. We have to trust that God is The One who will bring the dream to pass.

Commit your way to the Lord, Trust also in Him, And He will bring it to pass.[25]

If we don't learn to submit to God in our singleness, it will be extremely difficult to submit in marriage. It is so important to marry someone that is following the will of God, to know in submitting to him, we are actually submitting to God. A wife is a helpmate; we must be able to put our husbands needs' before our own, which is what Paul stated earlier; we should already be doing in Christ. We have to be the support that allows our husband and children to shine. Yes, God will allow His light to shine through us as virtuous women. The virtuous woman is praised for what she does for others; she is a support to her husband because he trusts safely in her. There are things he doesn't even have to worry about because he knows she has already taken care of her household, so he will have no lack of gain. She does her husband good and not evil, all the days of her life. She rises early to provide for her household. She is a successful businesswoman, negotiating deals and purchasing land. From her profits she doesn't go on an elaborate shopping spree; she reinvests her profits into a vineyard that will produce a harvest. She gives to the poor and gives a hand to those in need. Her household is well provided for and she walks in royal attire. Her husband is well-respected and she is optimistic about the days ahead.[26]

I am sure the virtuous woman did not live a life of ease without challenge, but she could laugh at days to come because she knew God's faithfulness. Regardless of the current situation, our God has the power to turn it around in the blink of an eye and even if He doesn't, He is still worthy to be praised. We must persevere in prayer before we see the change or are changed. Sometimes the situation doesn't change, but He changes us, and things we thought we needed would actually have harmed us. I thank God for the answered prayer, but also for the prayers that He did not answer for a particular job or relationship. Had I had my way, it would not have been for my good. His word tells us that the blessings of the Lord make one rich and adds no sorrow.[27] God is the only one that can know the end from the beginning, and we must trust that He has our best interests at heart.

Her children rise up and call her blessed; Her husband also, and he praises her; 'Many daughters have done well, But you excel them all. Charm is deceitful and beauty is passing. But a woman who fears the Lord, she shall be praised.[28]

When we don't walk in fear of the Lord, we just walk in fear. Desperate Debra has placed man in a role only God should have in our lives. Her fear of being alone has caused her to take the lead role in pursuing a relationship. Her soul focus is how she can please men, who will in return provide for her need to be loved. It is a very natural need Debra has but she must begin to trust God to be the provider. Instead of her desperately searching for a man, she must trust that God will provide her husband. While she is single, she must devote her time and attention to pleasing God and He will provide everything else. Too Through Tina is also taking the lead role because she has lost faith in God. We often don't realize that when we place our trust in our own ability, it is actually a loss of faith in God. Our fear of being let down, causes us to feel we must do everything ourselves or it won't get done. God would love to give Tina rest, but she has to trust Him to hold her hand.

Rest in the LORD, and wait patiently for Him.[29]

Resting in Him

We all would agree that we would enjoy the peace and rejuvenation that comes from being rested. When we think of all the demands on our lives, it becomes hard to stop to get the rest we need, not only physically, but mentally and spiritually. Jesus tells us to cast are cares upon Him for He cares for us and wants to give us rest. It is impossible to rest without trusting completely in God. I remember praying for God to help me put my life in His order and alignment. He answered my prayer in a very unexpected way. He stopped me dead in my tracks. I found out that I would have to have foot surgery and would not be able to drive for three weeks and full recovery would take months. All I could think about was all the things I needed to do and already had planned. I had to learn to submit my plans to His plan. They say it takes at least 21 days to begin to form a new habit. I knew that God would begin to do a new work in me during this time. The first week I was in so much pain all I could do was rest and pray for God's healing. By the second week I not only felt physically better, God began pouring ideas in to me for this book. I had set aside time to write before the surgery, but there always seemed like there was never enough time. As I spent unlimited quiet time with God, I could hear Him more clearly and the words just poured out of me. During the months of recuperation I was able to write freely. There were so many things that I thought I would miss out on, but God gave me so much more in Him.

Many times we are unable to rest or hear from God because our mind is clouded with so many concerns. I can't remember what I was worried about a year ago today, but I'm sure at the time it seemed so important. Many of the things we are concerned about distract us from seeking

God's perfect will for that day. Can you remember leaving the house and wondering whether or not you turned off the coffee pot, toaster, curling iron and just knowing that an electrical fire would breakout at any moment? You can literally see your house engulfed in flames. When you get home you see that all your worry was for naught, because you did, in fact, remember all along. Something as small as turning off an electrical appliance can distract your entire day. Until we are able to rest in God and trust Him to direct our day, we will continually have false alarms of worry that consume our mind and distract us from His purpose. When we look back on situations where we truly didn't know how we were going to make it, we can reflect on how God carried us through. It may not have looked or felt good at the time, but God had already worked it out.

We cannot allow phantom fears to paralyze our faith. Hesitant Heather is afraid to step out because she can't see past her fears. Do you find yourself asking, "What if I remain single for the rest of my life?" What if I don't have children or grandchildren? What if the person I am engaged to is not the one? What if my worst fears came true? We could go on for hours thinking about all the "what ifs" or we could begin to focus on what is. What is true is that God has a hope and a future for your life. What is true is that all things will work together for your good when you are called according to His purpose. The enemy will always try to rob you of your peace by challenging your position of faith. Regardless of how impossible the situation appears, is anything too hard for God? So often we allow ourselves to become paralyzed with fear and distracted from our purpose in God. As singles, it is so crucial that we remain focused on what God has called us to in this season of our lives. If we continue to wait for something to happen or not happen, we will miss out on what is happening.

God has already provided for everything we need. We cannot fathom the magnificence of God's eternal riches and His glory fills the earth. So we must ask ourselves, "Why am I worried?" God promises that when we delight ourselves in Him, He will give us the desires of our heart. Yet, we often want God to give us the desires of our heart, now, and then we promise to praise Him. However, if He gave us our desires before we learned to be content in Him alone, we would begin to worship the object of our desire more than God. Yet, when we are content to love God with all our heart, mind, and soul regardless of whether we get what we want or not, God will then bless us, knowing that our love for Him reigns supreme.

Throughout the Bible you will see various situations where God tests the faith and trust of His servants. I used to wonder why God would allow Abraham to come to the moment of death in the sacrifice of his beloved son Isaac. God could have provided the ram at the bottom of the mountain or He could have stopped Abraham before he bound Isaac to the altar. Yet, he waited to the very point of death with Abraham's knife lifted in the air in anticipation of sacrificing his greatest blessing from God. The angel of the Lord says to Abraham, "for **now** I know that you fear God, seeing that you have not withheld thy son, thine only son from me."[30] Then God confirmed how greatly He would bless Abraham and his seed. Lonely Lauri may wonder why God allowed her fiancé to marry someone else or why it appears that God has placed her in a situation that seemed to be the exact opposite of what He had promised. It is at this point that God knows whether she will trust Him completely.

Many times, we say we trust God but we are really

relying on our own strength and abilities. I remember when I had just finished graduate school and was confident that I would have a good job immediately after graduation. It was months before I found a job. I said to myself, I could volunteer until I started working full time. I was so hurt when the nursing home where I went to volunteer, stated they already had enough help. I couldn't believe the nursing home rejected me; it seemed liked doors were closing all around me. Sometimes God has to allow us to be rejected in order for us to be available to Him. Though I had faith that God would provide, I was still influenced by the mentality of the world that if you go to school, and especially graduate school, you are guaranteed a good job. Some of my faith was in my education and background, but God allowed me to see that everything I have is from Him alone. I can't take any credit or look for validation from people. He even allowed me to go through a season where I didn't get paid for a couple of months on my job, but I still went to work and tithed at my church. God allowed me to see that He is truly Jehovah Jireh, my provider. When I do get married, my faith will still be in God to provide for all of our needs. Many women go into marriage putting all their faith in their husband. However, after the loss of my father at thirteen, my mother had to take full responsibility for our household. If she had put her faith in my father and not in God, she would have been devastated. Though it was difficult, our faith in God was only strengthened as we saw how God could make a way out of no way.

God has not given us a spirit of fear, but of power, love and a sound mind. We must stay focused on His will and put our faith completely in Him. When we trust in Him with all our hearts and lean not to our own understanding, but acknowledge Him in all our ways, He promises that He will direct our path. We never have to fear when we know God has led us in our path, regardless of how difficult or hopeless it may appear; God sees the glorious ending and by faith we can see it, too. When we are willing to sacrifice our own agenda on the altar, then our fears are replaced with faith. When we become consumed in meeting God's needs, we can rest assured that He will make sure our needs are met. When we learn to serve God wholeheartedly in our singleness, then He will know that we will continue to serve Him in marriage, in our careers, and in all that we do. We will see how God is able to do so much more than we could do on our own.

Pushing Through Pain

We often feel like giving up when we face obstacles in pursuing what God has for us, but we have to learn to push through the pain. When people are working out, they know "No pain, no gain." The same principle that applies to physical growth of muscle applies to our spiritual growth. If even Jesus had to endure pain in order for Him to fulfill the Father's plan for His life, why would we be exempt? In the Garden of Gethsemane, Jesus pushed through the pain stating, "Oh, My Father, if it is possible let this cup pass from Me; nevertheless, not as I will, but as You will."[31] We, too, must come to the conclusion that ultimately we want the perfect will of God for our lives, even if it involves pain. If it weren't for the pain, we wouldn't realize how strong we actually are in God and how faithful He is to deliver us. We also appreciate the good times much more. There are people who live with chronic pain and when God delivers them from that pain, they have a much greater appreciation of God than a person who has never experienced that degree of pain. I know women who went through such a painful relationship, but they are blessed with such a wonderful marriage now that they don't even think about the pain of yesterday.

When I think of the epitome of a woman in the Bible that pushed through the pain to get her blessing, I have to acknowledge the woman with the issue of blood. For twelve long years she dwelt with the rejection and pain her condition caused. We never know the full extent of her pain, but it is said that she suffered many things. We know she was not able to enter the temple according to Jewish law, she was shunned by family, friends, and even church members. She had lost all her material wealth as she struggled to find a cure for her illness. Though the situation appeared hopeless, she knew there was still hope. There was One who had not forsaken her. No matter what it cost her financially, physically, emotionally, or spiritually, she would push through to touch the only One that could heal her, Jesus Christ. She didn't beg and plead with Jesus, she simply touched the hem of his garment, knowing she would be made whole. Immediately, she received her healing and Jesus told her, "Daughter, your faith has made you well. Go in peace and be healed of your affliction."[32] Jesus was not moved by her words, He was compelled to respond to her faith. We must understand that we can cry ourselves to sleep every night and nothing will happen, but the minute we push through by faith, God has to respond to our situation. He tells us in His word,

And whatever things you ask in prayer, believing, you will receive.[33]

I think we sometimes look at the woman with the issue of blood and think that, that situation was then, but it is irrelevant today. I am here to tell you that God is still a healer. Whether it is physical or emotional healing that needs to take place, there is nothing too hard for God. I would not even be here today if it weren't for the miraculous healing power of God. Just like the woman with the issue of blood, my own mother had severe problems with bleeding during her cycle from the time she was a teenager. When she was just a teenager, doctors wanted to perform a hysterectomy, which would have prevented her from ever having children. Thank God my grandparents were people of faith who did not agree to the hysterectomy. They did however, put her on birth control pills that were still experimental during that time. The pills were at such a dosage, my mother almost died. She did recover by God's grace. When my mother married my father, doctors still believed that she would never have any children. Obviously, God had other plans and blessed her with my older brother and then a beautiful baby girl. I say that to say don't put your trust in what other people are saying, know that if God said it, He will perform it even when it seems impossible.

Virtuous Victoria had been told it would be impossible to remain abstinent until the day of her marriage. Michael had always pressured her to prove her love to him, by giving him the most precious gift she could give - her virginity. She knew that if he really loved her with the love of Christ, he would have never put her in that position. Victoria began to realize that her relationship with Michael was not based on love, but on lust. It wasn't about what he could give to her, but what he could take for himself. When she left Michael, she prayed to God to give her the strength to not only abstain from sex, but to walk as a woman of virtue in every area and not even give the appearance of immorality in her life. When she met Kevin, it was refreshing to see a man that shared her desire to please God at all times, not just on Sunday. She respected him as her friend not knowing that one day he would become her husband. Though the wait was challenging and rejection was painful, God had answered Victoria's prayer for a godly husband.

Whatever you are believing God to do in your life, know that you have not been forgotten. He has heard your prayer and He has seen every tear. There is no good gift that He will withhold from you. He desires to bless you, but we must wait on His timing. Sometimes we want the right thing at the wrong time. To everything there is a season and we must wait for the appointed time for our blessing. In the meantime, we must walk as women of virtue and honor, rejoicing in the hope of our salvation.

Prayer

Lord, forgive me for the times I have tried to take my life into my own hands. I give my life to you to use for your glory. Shape me and mold me in your image. I know that you have already prepared everything I will ever need. I will trust you to provide for me in every area of my life. Thank you for sending me people to show me your faithfulness and hold me accountable to your word. I thank you for godly relationships that help me to push through the pain and become healed and whole in You. I cast my cares upon You, for I know you care for me. I thank you for allowing me to rest in you. I will be still and know that You alone are God. Amen.

Chapter Three
Our Direction

Trust in the Lord with all your heart, and lean not to your own understanding; In all your ways acknowledge Him, and He shall direct your paths. Do not be wise in your own eyes; Fear the Lord and depart from evil.[34]

Purposeful Planning

If you have ever purchased home assembly furniture, toys, or other products, they always come with an instruction manual. Sometimes in my haste, I don't want to bother reading the instruction manual; I just want to get right to work. I usually have several other things to do and this is just one more item on my to-do list to finish as quickly as possible. Inevitably, a screw will end up in the wrong place or something does not fit and as a last resort I must turn to the manual for instructions. When we have an instruction manual, it's important that we take time to read it carefully. I remember putting a desk together with my mother and at the end, it wasn't very sturdy. We read the manual, but somehow there were extra pieces left over. We reinforced it with additional nails at the end, but it never became what the designer had initially planned. Our Creator is truly the only one who can reveal to us what His plans are for our lives. We must carefully read His instruction manual and follow His direction for us to fulfill His perfect will for our lives. The verse above instructs us to give all our plans to God from the beginning and trust Him completely to bring the plan to pass. The problem arises when we feel that we are wise enough to figure it out all on our own. The virtuous woman who fears the Lord will be praised, but when we disregard God's instruction, we are setting ourselves up for failure and disgrace. Yes, there are women who have benefited from the temporary satisfaction of ill-gotten gains, but what does it benefit us to gain the whole world and lose our soul. God wants to bless us, but we must be willing to do things in His order.

At times, we can clearly see when something was not done in proper order. I have always enjoyed baking and the order in which ingredients are added can affect the texture, flavor, or taste. I could never understand how someone could take the same recipe for a delicious cake and end up with a gooey mess. Though they had the instructions, they clearly did not follow them. They decided to adapt the recipe to their liking, but it did not turn out the same. Sometimes, we want to adapt God's word to meet our needs and wonder why we don't see the promised results. How many times in our lives has God given us clear directions, but we alter His word, ever so slightly to fit our agenda? At the end we realize our shortcut took us completely off course, and learn we should have followed His directions from the beginning. An even slight deviation from His word puts us off course and in a place of disobedience.

As we look at the life of the virtuous woman, we see that she is responsible in many areas spiritually, relationally, financially, and socially. This doesn't just occur by happen stance. As she understands her role and walks in the fear of the Lord, she is able to align her priorities with God's will for her life. We have to spend time with God in order for Him to show us His divine plan for our lives. We must make sure our plans are in sync with His plans. The virtuous woman rises early to start her day. It is so important that we are able to seek God early to reveal His will for that day. All throughout the Bible, we are provided examples of men and women of God who rose early to seek the Lord's will. We, too, must realize that we are much more productive when we look at the instruction manual from the beginning. God tells us to seek Him for wisdom and He will give it liberally, without reproach.[35] Instead of coming to God at the end of the day, when we have placed things out of order or tried to make things fit on our own, we can review his instruction manual and seek His wisdom from the start.

Sometimes, we see spending time with God as just another item on our To-Do list. However, we must cherish the quiet time we have to spend with our Lord as precious and holy. We shouldn't enjoy spending time with anyone else more than with God. If you were told that you had the opportunity to meet one of your all time favorite actors or singers, you would rise up at four o'clock in the morning if necessary. We shouldn't see rising a little early to spend time with the Creator of the Universe as an inconvenience. The unfortunate thing is we often spend time religiously and not relationally. The maker of the heavens and the earth, our Father, the Creator, wants to spend meaningful time with us. We often come to God with a To-Do list of our goals for that day and are off on our way, never taking the time to seek His will or to be still and hear His plans for our day. It's hard to believe that God is mindful of every aspect of our lives and knows the plans He has for us each day. David, known as a man after God's own heart, stated,

THE ONE

When I consider Your heavens, the work of your fingers,
The moon and the stars, which You have ordained, What
is man that you are mindful of him, And the son of man
that You visit him?[36]

God is such a gentleman that He would stand at the door and ask to spend time with us. We are never forced or coerced to take the invitation. What an honor to be pursued by The One. I recently saw a movie where a young girl was struggling in her faith and her parent's new found relationship with Christ. She went on a trip just to get away from everything. She ended up sitting next to a man who was a counselor and she started sharing all her problems with a complete stranger. He listened intently and gave advice and examples when needed. At the end of her flight, it seemed as if this kind stranger disappeared into thin air and she realized she had just had an encounter with Jesus. Once she realized the depth of God's love for her, she gave her life to Christ and reconnected with her parents. I wonder if there are times when we encounter the spirit of a loving God and do not even acknowledge Him. He desires to spend time with us, but we must be willing to receive Him.

Receive, Believe, and Conceive

Just as we receive Christ into our hearts, we must continue to invite Him to be a part of every aspect of our lives. He is always available, but we must allow His presence to come in. I think we often take His presence for granted and go about our day without acknowledging our very best friend. Sometimes, we do ask for God's guidance, but we do not want to receive and embrace what He has called us to do. If we reject His will, we will continually find ourselves not satisfied or fulfilled. Hesitant Heather is completely dissatisfied with every aspect of her life. She would rather hold on to what she knows than to receive God's word that He has more for her life. She looks at her plans to have her own business and travel the world as a dream, but has never truly believed it could be possible. Though she recites in church that all things are possible through Christ that strengthens her, she has not lived it out in her everyday life.

Just like Mary, we have to be willing to receive the word of God regardless of the consequences. When Gabriel, the angel of God, came to Mary and told her that she was favored by God and was chosen to bring forth the Son of God, Mary had to decide whether to receive the word of God or dismiss it as impossible, since she was still a virgin. How do we know it is truly a word from God? If you can do it on your own, you may want to spend some time sorting out if it is truly His will or your will. If you can make it happen all on your own, then where is God? God's word always stretches us beyond our own ability. If His ways are not our ways and His thoughts higher than our thoughts, His word is going to be bigger than what our natural mind can conceive. It will require divine intervention. When Mary was told she would become pregnant, she initially asked Gabriel, "How could this be, since I do not know a man?"[37] Gabriel explained that this pregnancy would be consummated spiritually for the Holy Spirit would come upon her. He also reminded her of her relative Elizabeth who was thought to be barren but now will conceive. Mary received the word of God and believed that it was true stating, "Behold the maidservant of the Lord. Let it be to me according to your word."[38] Mary completely surrendered herself to allow the will of God to be conceived in and through her, even though receiving the word would mean that she would not only face being rejected by strangers, but also by her own fiancé. You may be looking at what appears to be an impossible situation in your business, finances, family, or health. I will say to you as the angel said to Mary, "For with God nothing will be impossible."[39] He will open doors and provide provisions you would have never imagined to be possible.

You must first receive the word to be true for you. It's easy to believe God can work it out for someone else, but you must know that He is working it out for you. When we receive the word and believe it is real in our lives, then we can begin to prepare to conceive. Just as a woman prepares for the birth of her baby, we must prepare for the things God has given us to birth. Mary was highly favored as she was spiritually ready to receive the blessing of God. Because she was a virgin, it was truly an immaculate conception. She had consecrated her life to Him and walked in righteousness. In order for us to walk in the fullness of God's blessing, we still must walk in righteousness. God still wants us to honor Him with our body. We must be spiritually prepared to receive the blessings of God. With great excitement and anticipation, we must continue to pursue the things for which we have been called to give birth. Women must go through a season of purification before and during the pregnancy. Many adjustments should be made in her diet, her lifestyle, and her behavior. In order to protect and provide for the baby, the mother may have to give up smoking, drinking, using drugs; even some prescriptions may be harmful. Activities that may have been fine before the pregnancy could potentially be harmful now. Physically, she will need to refrain from strenuous activities and be able to rest. Just as a woman prepares for a physical birth, she must prepare for a spiritual breakthrough. God will require you to abstain from sex, drugs, or drinking so you will not stunt your spiritual growth. We don't want our actions to abort the work of God in our lives. We may experience some pain, the additional weight of His glory, and some fatigue, but we must know, that in our weakness, God is strong. As we make plans, when it is our season to deliver, we will be prepared for the blessing. We will not be caught off guard and we will be able to sustain the life of that blessing. Once the blessing arrives, then the real work begins. It must be nurtured and cared for continually. There will be sleepless nights and selfless sacrifices, but there will also be a joy that is greater than any pain. A sense of peace and fulfillment will come from being in a place of favor and blessing. Our God will do exceedingly and abundantly more than we ever thought was possible when we stand on His word. When we feel like giving up, we have to keep standing, knowing that there is a greater blessing on the other side. We must not settle for anything less than God's best.

Not allowing feelings to steal your faith

It is not a matter of feelings. Romans 1:17 says, "The righteousness of God is revealed from faith to faith; as it is written, 'The just shall live by faith'." Believe God for your marriage. It will not be your feelings that heal your relationship. It will be your faith!" [40] T. D. Jakes

During pregnancy and during certain times of the month in preparation for a possible pregnancy, it is easy for our emotions to get the best of us. The slightest incidence can cause a flood of tears and emotion. As our body is going through physical changes, our emotional homeostasis is thrown in a tizzy. As we are birthing a spiritual breakthrough, we must not allow our feelings to get the best of us, as we wait for the manifestation of what God has promised. Regardless of how we are feeling, we have to remember that God is faithful. When we make decisions based on how we are feeling and not by faith, we often end up giving up or settling for less than God's best. Because we are seeking a temporary balm for our pain, when we allow God to be our balm in Gilead, He will give us joy for sorrow and beauty for ashes. Our feelings can lead us into a downward spiral of self-pity, shame, and depression. However, when we give praise while we wait on God, He gives us hope, strength, and patience. I remember telling God that I was tired of worrying about this or that and He whispered in my spirit, "Then don't worry and know that it is already done in me." When we really trust God to do what He says He will do, there is nothing left to worry about. It is impossible to walk in doubt or low self-esteem when we realize who lives within us. We can do all things through Christ who strengthens us, when we remember it is He who gives us strength. As single women, we often feel like everything is on our shoulders, like there is no one to turn to. It was God, who blessed us with the job to pay the bills. So why worry about things we know our Father will provide.

Hesitant Heather will never be able to walk in God's promises until she learns to completely trust in God. She has allowed low self-esteem and fear to rob her of an abundant life. Not only is her life affected, but also the people God wants to use her to bless. The enemy knows that if he can keep us in bondage, he can keep us from reaching all the people God wants our lives to touch. We have to realize that our families, our children, our communities, our world can be released from bondage by seeing us walk in to our destiny. They can begin to believe God to help them walk into their destiny. Lonely Lauri and Busy Brittany are also dealing with issues of fear, by not allowing God to have full control in their lives. Lauri would always break off relationships and quit jobs because of her fear of rejection. On the other hand, Brittany's schedule is so tight there is no room for God to intervene. We have to step back and ask God to take over. When He does, there is no need for us to fear - He has our very best interests at heart.

Do not fear, for you will not be ashamed; Neither be disgraced, for you will not be put to shame; For you will forget the shame of your youth, And will not remember the reproach of your widowhood anymore. For your Maker is your husband, The Lord of hosts is His name. [41]

Regardless of how it may look, when we stand on faith God will not allow us to be put to shame. It may seem like everything is about to fall apart, but don't allow your feelings to deceive you. Our God is our redeemer and provider. Though we may not be married in the natural, spiritually, we are God's bride. There is no need, that He does not have the ability to supply. When He supplies the need it is so much better than anything we could have done on our own. You may be able to pay the bill, but He can pay off the bill. I remember when my grandmother was in the hospital, there was an enormous hospital bill that would take my mother a lifetime to pay off. After my grandmother passed and my mother called about the bill, the woman responded, "What bill?" My mother tried to explain to her about the bill she knew existed. She realized by God's grace, somehow the bill was paid off. If she would have walked in fear and avoided the bill, she would have never seen God show up in a miraculous way and provide. It was good for my mother to try to pay some of the bill, but God had something better in mind. What's good may not always be what is best.

Is it good or is it God?

I think the hardest things to give to God are not the things we could live without but the things that really seem good, but may stand in the way of God's best. I know when I was deciding whether to leave my former employer it was a difficult decision. It's hard to leave a job you actually enjoy and people you care about. I loved my co-workers and my students, but I knew God wanted more for my life. There was something bigger, than where I was, something greater to accomplish. However, what we believe to be good is determined by our experiences. Once we experience something greater, what we thought was good is not as good as we thought. Sometimes, God will pull you from associations and relationships not necessarily because they are bad, but because He wants you to grow. God often isolates us in order to have our full attention. We don't realize that we have been distracted by so many good intentions. We have to ask is it good or is it God? Yes, God is good, but all good things aren't God. Things that appear bad do not tempt us; it is the things that appear good that can throw us off track.

When Eve was tempted in the garden, she saw that the tree was "good for food, that it was pleasant to the eyes, and a tree desirable to make one wise." [42]

It appeared that the fruit would be good for her and her husband, but it was not in line with God's word. God did not tempt them, but their own desire led to sin and separation from God. Even Virtuous Victoria was almost drawn away by her desire to be with a fine man. Michael was fine and a good man, but He was not who God sent. She could allow herself to believe that God must have sent this fine man in her life, just as Eve had allowed the serpent to be deceive her into believing that what appeared good, must be God. I know many good-looking brothers who may even have good intentions, but it still does not mean he is the one God has ordained. Though you may desire a husband, do not allow your desire to be loved to separate you from God's perfect love. Many women are living with men whom they desire to be their husbands, but statistics show that co-habitation more often does not lead to marriage and, more importantly, it doesn't line up with God's perfect will. Every gift that comes from God will be good and will lead us into His perfect will. Do not be deceived, my sisters, every good and perfect gift comes from our Father. [43]

Mary sought to please The One over the one and God spoke to Joseph in a dream so that he would not reject her. When we trust God with everything, He will give us everything we need to fulfill His will for our lives. We shouldn't be surprised when it feels like we are being tested in every area; that is how we know God is perfecting us and preparing us for more. When we are tested in every area and we pass the test, it also shows God that we trust Him in every area. Testing may be a result of your faithfulness. God allowed the enemy to test Job because of his righteousness. He then blessed Job with much more than he had before the test and God was glorified as people witnessed his faithfulness through the test. If you are not being stretched or challenged, then you may need to ask if you are truly walking in God's will. We must have the faith to risk everything in order to gain everything. It is not God's will for us to lack any good thing. He wants us to be whole and complete in Him. We must allow ourselves to be stripped of everything, in order to walk in the fullness of His blessing. Sometimes when it looks like we are going down, God is really raising us up.

Count it all joy when you fall into various trials, knowing the testing of your faith produces patience. But let patience have its perfect work, that you may be perfect and complete, lacking nothing. [44]

Prayer

Lord, lead and guide my steps by your word. Help me to know your perfect will for my life. Teach me to trust you through the trials I may face. I receive the word that you have spoken over my life. I believe that I will become who you have called me to be. I will conceive the plans you have birthed within me. Regardless of the obstacles I may face, I trust you. Regardless of the sacrifices I may have to make, I trust you. Regardless of the pain I may take, I trust you. Thank you for giving me wisdom to know the difference between what may appear good, and what is God ordained for my life. I know you are working all things together for my good because I love you and am committed to your purpose.

Chapter Four
Presenting God Our Whole Heart

Blessed are those who keep His testimonies, Who seek Him with the whole heart! [45]

Too through Tina has been so hurt by previous relationships her heart had become hardened by pain and bitterness. The only one that has the power to soften Tina's heart to receive true love is God. Unfortunately, she has trouble giving her heart completely to God. She is so tired of broken promises; she thinks God will let her down as well. One thing she must remember is that God's promises are sure. He is the only One who can see the end from the beginning. I know women who God has given awesome blessings to out of tremendous pain. Women that went through abusive relationships and thought they would never find real love were blessed with amazing men of God.

One of these women was my grandmother. At a time when divorce was looked upon with disdain, my grandmother was able to maintain her dignity after going through an abusive marriage. She went back to school, became a nurse and took care of her two sons. Later she would meet a handsome, godly man who would shower her with unconditional love. In this union she would give birth to my mother, who would later give birth to a son and a daughter. What if she had given up on love? She would never have been able to receive my grandfather's love and subsequently not had my mother. My mother would not have had me and my brother. My grandmother was truly a joy to be around. Despite the trials she had endured, she never lost her joy and love for life. Though my grandfather had passed away before I was born, my mother continues to share with her children what an amazing father and husband he was to his family. Many women feel that they a man will not love their children from a previous marriage, but my grandfather adopted my grandmother's sons and gave them his name. They were always treated as his own sons. God is able to do so much more than we could ever imagine. We must be willing to open our hearts to Him completely, so He can heal us and restore us by His grace.

We often believe that we are giving God our whole heart, when we are keeping sections of our heart from God. We believe God in one area, but hold back in other areas. How do we know if we are holding back from God? A good sign of what we are holding back is usually found in the areas of our lives where we feel fearful, anxious, impatient, angry, or unforgiving. If you are in a relationship where you continually find yourself in fear that you may lose the other or anxious about what others are saying, you may have placed that relationship before your relationship with God. In God, there is perfect peace, fullness of joy, and unconditional love. Many times we are not even aware that we are holding onto certain areas. I remember being at a women's conference several years ago and recognizing a feeling of sadness that was unexplainable. It appeared to come from nowhere. My pastor, Bishop Eddie L. Long, began to make a call for forgiveness and as I began to ask God to take away the sadness I felt. God began to reveal areas from my childhood where I had not completely forgiven. When I gave those areas to God, I felt such an overwhelming feeling of joy and peace. I have never felt that feeling of sadness ever again. I know that had I carried that with me, there would have continued to be an area of my heart that was not yielded completely to God.

Many times, we carry pain and hurt into future relationships, always upset with the other person but never realizing that it's really someone in your past that must be forgiven. Many times when children distrust their mother or father, they find it hard to trust their spouse in marriage. They always feel that if they let their guard down for just a minute, they will be hurt or disappointed. The fact of the matter is that there will always be people that will hurt or disappoint us, but that is no reason to stop living. When we allow God to be God, we can allow people to be people. I believe that we will receive what we believe. If we believe that all men are no good, don't be surprised if you find yourself with a no-good man. It may actually be a good man, but if that is what you continually speak that is all you will see and eventually what he becomes. Too Through Tina only receives what she expects from men – hurt and betrayal. When she is able to fully open her heart to God, she will then discover a joy and love that will fill the dark hole of pain she has tried to fill with man's love, but can only be filled by God's love. Jeremiah reveals that our hearts are deceitful and it is hard to know what is truly in our hearts. We can deceive ourselves to believe that everything is good, when pride, envy, bitterness, or anger could be hiding inside of our hearts. We will always attract like spirits. So if you wonder why you always seem to attract negative people, you may need to begin to look internally instead of at other people externally. As God is perfecting us, we continually must ask God to refine our hearts and remove anything that would hinder us from receiving the fullness of Christ's love for us.

The Lord desires to bless us, but our lack of forgiveness can create a blockage that prevents the free flow of his blessings. It's like a hardening of the arteries that is clogged with fatty deposits that constrict the blood from reaching the heart. Eventually, it may cause a heart attack or even death. Just like our physical heart, our spiritual heart can become hardened by bitterness and unforgiveness. Our Great Physician is able to remove the blockage in our spiritual hearts. The blood of Christ cleanses us from all impurity. It's ironic that high cholesterol is not only caused by diet, but also by heredity and stress. Our diet may also be affected by stress. We tend to crave unhealthy fixes of fast food when we are under the crunch. Many people that have suffered from abuse also tend to use food, alcohol, or other substances as a form of self-medication. The problem is that we cannot heal ourselves or perform surgery on our own hearts. We must allow God to give us peace in stressful times and also allow us to forgive people for the pain they caused in our lives. When we allow God to heal our spiritual heart, we will find that our physical heart will heal as well.

Today if you will hear His voice, Do not harden your hearts. [46]

Tina must be able to see that God is not like man and all men are not like Tyrone. God still has an awesome plan to give her a hope and a future, but she will have to learn to trust Him again. God has heard her every prayer and though He may not have responded the way she would have liked, He never left her alone. Sometimes God allows others to reject us in order for His will to come to pass. If Jesus had not betrayed by Judas, He would not have been pushed into His destiny. We may feel as if we are dying, but that is the point where God can resurrect us to a greater level of glory. He is the one that has always provided for her, even during her marriage, and He continues to be her provider as a single-mother. We must not allow the pain of the past to harden our hearts.

Though David was known as a "man after God's own heart," he too had to ask God's forgiveness and ask God to purify his heart. David prayed God,

Create in me a clean heart and to renew a steadfast spirit within me. [47]

David knew what God desired from him most was a broken spirit and a contrite or repentant heart. When we hold onto unforgiveness, bitterness, and pain our hearts become hardened, but when we give it to God He is able to heal us and give us a heart of flesh again. We cannot allow pride to keep us from surrendering our pain. We think if we keep it all the pain inside and act like nothing is wrong it will all be better. God desires our brokenness and complete surrender to His will. We must be willing to ask for His forgiveness and then we can forgive ourselves. It is then that we are able to fall back in love with our first love, our Lord and Savior. He is the only One that can save us. No earthly relationship will be ever fill the spiritual void that God fulfills in our lives. When we are so in love with God, then we will be free to love others unconditionally.

Freedom to Love

When we are able to give our hearts to God completely, it is then we are able to truly love others. Where the spirit of the Lord is, there is liberty. Many times we allow past heart breaks to bind us in fear, but perfect love casts out fear. The only One that can show us how to love with a perfect love is God. In society today, we use the word love so casually. "I love that movie" or "I love that song." Desperate Debra thought she was in love the moment she met both her first and second husband, but it seemed like once they were married the butterflies in her stomach seemed to fade away. She didn't feel like she was in love with him anymore and the relationship quickly turned sour. What Debra didn't understand was that the world's version of love is based on a feeling while God's perfect love is based on a decision. While we were yet sinners, He decided to love us by giving His only son to die in order to bring us back in relationship with Him. God's love is unconditional; it's not dependent upon our actions. I think of the prodigal son and how even though the son's actions were disappointing, the father never loved his son any less. When his son returned, he gave a celebration in his honor. Isn't it awesome to know that regardless of what we do, we are valuable in God's eyes. The moment we return back to His love, He wants to put us back in our rightful place. The world would want others to prove they deserve to be back in right standing, but not God. We hold grudges, but God just wants to hold our heart.

It is only through God that we are free to love others unconditionally, even if we do not receive what we desire from them. Of all our spiritual gifts the greatest gift we have been given is to love. Paul states that though he may have the gift of prophesy, or the gift of knowledge or even faith to move mountains, it means nothing without love. [48] He goes on to describe the characteristics of Godly love,

> *Love never gives up. Love cares more for others than for self. Love doesn't want what it doesn't have. Love doesn't strut, Doesn't have a swelled head, Doesn't force itself on others, Isn't always "me first," Doesn't fly off the handle, Doesn't keep score of the sins of others, Doesn't revel when others grovel, Takes pleasure in the flowering of truth, Puts up with anything, Trusts God always, Always looks for the best, Never looks back, But keeps going to the end. Love never dies.* [49]

I have rarely seen love like that portrayed in popular movies or television shows. In fact, in many cases the exact opposite characteristics of love is exemplified: impatience, jealousy, self-seeking, rejoicing in gossip, always looking for the worst, keeping record of every wrong, and is easily ended. Hesitant Heather is always thinking if I really loved wholeheartedly, my heart would be broken when it is not reciprocated. What if I get hurt? It must be possible to love too much? The word tells us to be anxious for nothing and as we give thanks, the peace of God, which goes beyond comprehension, will guard our hearts and minds through Christ Jesus.[50] The best way for us to guard our hearts is to give it completely to God and He will protect us and keep us in perfect peace. That is truly freedom to love - to not have to worry about whether or not we will be hurt. Jesus knew He would be hurt and rejected, yet He still loved. Above all He loved His Father more than anything else. We have to come to a place where we love our Father so much that there is nothing that anyone can do to take away our joy. God loves us so much and only wants His best for us. Every promise given by God will be fulfilled. We don't have to worry about if it will come to pass, but simply prepare ourselves for when it will come to pass.

Blessed is she who believed, for there will be a fulfillment of those things, which were told her from the Lord.[51]

Regardless of what has happened in the past, keep dreaming and keep believing that all things are still possible because they truly are possible in Christ. Even though the promise seems to be delayed, you will not be denied. God's word has come to pass, so if He said it, it's going to happen. Prepare for the promise and continue to know that God has not forgotten you. Wherever we are, we must learn to enjoy the process. As Paul, states, we must learn to be content in every situation. We may not be where we want to be, but we're not where we were, Amen. It takes years of pressure and intense heat for a lump of coal to become a diamond. God is allowing the pressure of life to prepare us to shine brilliantly for Him. When we think of where God has brought us from, it keeps us humble. We know it was by His love, His grace, His peace – that we have become purified as pure gold. His love will sustain us through every season.

Falling in Love with Our First Love

*Nevertheless I have this against you, that you have left your **first love**.*[52]

Paul also speaks to the church of Ephesus in Ephesians. He reminds them from where God has brought them from. Though they were once dead in sin, fulfilling the desires of their flesh, by God's grace they have been given the gift of life.[53] Paul commends them for all their many good works, but reminds them that it was by grace that they have been saved through faith. Perhaps the Ephesians began to boast of their great works, but Paul reminds them how far God has brought them. We all must continually remember where God has brought us from, in order to rekindle our passion for God. We can begin to think that it is our work with the homeless, our teaching of the Word, or serving on the usher board, that presents us as righteous. By faith, God has presented us with His righteousness and by His grace we are saved. When we think of the goodness of God, you can't help but to fall in love with Him all over again. Paul prays that God will ground the Ephesians in love, that they would know the width and length and depth and height of God's awesome love.[54] As we begin to understand the magnitude of God's love for us, the more we should desire to please Him. If that is not enough, if we were to think about where our lives would be without Him, we will have the power to walk away from anything that would break His heart. As I am writing this, Israel Houghton's song begins to play stating: "Where would I be, if not for your grace." Even as you are reading this, stop for a moment and begin to think of all the things that God has brought you out of, delivered you from, and carried you through.

I look behind me and you're there,
then up ahead and you're there, too—
your reassuring presence, coming and going.
This is too much, too wonderful—
I can't take it all in![55]

Paul warns us that it is important for us to guard our relationship with God and not allow anything to taint our relationship or keep us from our inheritance in Christ. We must be careful that we do not even give the appearance that we are unfaithful in our relationship with Him. Paul states, "But fornication and all uncleanness or covetousness, let it not even be named among you, as is fitting for the saints; neither filthiness, nor foolish talking, nor coarse jesting."[56]   We have to be mindful that our relationship is a testimony of our faith. As single women we must be careful that we are aware of the mixed messages our actions could be presenting. When others know that you are staying the night over at a boyfriend's house, even though nothing sexual happened, it could give the appearance that something did. Our actions should glorify God so that others may see our good works and glorify our Father as well. Yes, there will always be people who will try to condemn you for no reason, but let's not give them justification. They tried to condemn Jesus, but He was found faultless in all His ways. Paul reminds us to walk with caution, not foolishly, making the most of the time we are given. As singles, it is so important that we are not careless with this time we have been given. God has anointed us for specific assignments in this season; it is crucial that we keep God first in our hearts and are not distracted. Sometimes we must rededicate our lives back to God or perhaps we never really gave God our whole heart. In that case, we need to repent. Ask Jesus to come into our hearts, confess Him as our Lord and Savior, and change our lives for His glory, realizing that when we ask Him for forgiveness, He no longer remembers the sin, so there is now no condemnation for those in Christ Jesus.

THE ONE

Prayer

Lord, I thank you for your unconditional love in my life. I am able to forgive those who have rejected me because I don't want anything to keep me from giving you my whole heart. Lord, I surrender my whole heart to you. Come into my heart and purify my life. Create in me a clean heart and renew a right spirit within me. You desire a broken spirit and a contrite heart. Lord forgive me for anything I have done to break your heart. You are my first love. You are my peace. You give me fullness of joy. Thank you for being my first love. Thank you for loving me and choosing me to be yours, even when I rejected you. I love you Lord. I thank you for allowing everything I have endured to prepare me to shine as a precious diamond for you. Not my will, but your will be done in my life. Amen.

THE ONE

Chapter Five
Giving God Our Best

But this I say: He who sows sparingly will also reap sparingly, and he who sows bountifully will also reap bountifully. So let each one give as he purposes in his heart, not grudgingly or of necessity; for God loves a cheerful giver.[57]

One temptation we must be careful to avoid as single women is the tendency to become self-centered, only focused on our wants, desires, or needs and not taking the time to help others meet their goals. Sometimes it's really an unconscious mindset that comes from being the sole provider of your household, the owner of your company. We can easily become so consumed in the day-to-day grind that we don't realize that we have unintentionally shut others out of our lives. Yes, our single years should be a time to invest in ourselves and our relationship with God. It also is a time when we can sow our gifts, talents, time, and resources. I have served in youth ministry for several years and though I am there to serve them, they give me the greatest gifts. The one thing I like about working with youth is that there is no pretense with them. They say whatever is on their mind. If you have kids of your own, they will show you areas where you may need more patience, more understanding, or more trust.

My students teach me just as much if not more than I

teach them. As a college professor, I have seen students that have overcome tremendous adversity and still have joy. I have seen young people battling terminal illness, yet still do well in school. They continually show me new ways to look at ideas or problems. It is truly a privilege to serve them. No, it's not always easy, but it is rewarding to know that you have played a small part in helping them to reach their goals. There are gifts and talents that God has given you to be a blessing to someone else. You will find that as you give of your gifts freely, you will get back more than you have given.

Everyday we have the opportunity to be a student in the classroom of life and there are so many lessons to be learned. It seems that we can learn the most when we step out of our world and our comfort zones to appreciate the life of another. Is that not what the Savior has done for us? He forsook the glory and honor of being with the Father to touch our lives. It's so much bigger than just our lives and our dreams. God loved us so much that He gave His only Son that we all might have eternal life. We too have something to give to this world. It may be with your family, your community, your church or it could be national or international. Only God can reveal the infinite possibilities He has placed within us. His plan for us is usually much bigger than our plan for ourselves.

I don't think the way you think.
The way you work isn't the way I work."
God's Decree.
"For as the sky soars high above earth,
so the way I work surpasses the way you work,
and the way I think is beyond the way you think.[58]

THE ONE

I am sure after the loss of her husband at a young age; Ruth did not initially see how God had a greater plan for her life. Ruth was willing to sow her life into the life of Naomi. Though Naomi encouraged her daughter in-law to leave, knowing that with both sons and her husband dead, there were little prospects of them marrying again if they stayed with her. Ruth begged her not to leave.

Where you go, I go; and where you live, I'll live. Your people are my people, your God is my god; where you die, I'll die, and that's where I'll be buried, so help me GOD— not even death itself is going to come between us![59]

Though Ruth came from a people who were despised by Jewish people for their sinful nature and worship of other Gods, somehow Ruth stands as a pillar of faithfulness and unconditional love. Though she may have desired to marry again, she was willing to deal with the possibility that there may not be any more prospects if she stayed with Naomi, but she would remain faithful until death. As she was sowing into someone else God blessed her for her faithfulness. Not only did he allow her to be provided for by marrying Boaz, but she kept her oath to Naomi and was able to provide for her as well. Who would believe that God would use this humble and faithful woman to help establish the lineage of Jesus Christ. The word tells us that when we lose our life, it is then that we gain life. When we are willing to forsake all for the will of God, it is then that we gain everything in Him.

After my father passed away there was one scripture my mother stood on, "I have never seen the righteous forsaken, nor their seed begging bread."[60] My mother didn't know if she would be able to keep our house on her own. She was told there would be no way that I would be able to go to college. Yet, I witnessed how she still remained faithful in giving to her church and others. She didn't try to run to another man to provide. She made a conscious decision that she would protect and cover me. God honored my mother for her faithful giving and for raising a standard of holiness in her home. As single women, it can be easy to justify not giving tithes. We must remember it is God that has given us the ability to work and it is He who has supplied our need, not our job. This is the one area that God tells us we can test Him and see how He will open the windows of heaven and pour out a blessing so big that we cannot receive it all.[61] He will also give us favor and prevent destruction from the enemy. Pastor Mike Hayes explained in his book, When God is First, how our tithe or tenth is given first in order that the blessing rest on the ninety percent. When we put God first in everything, including our finances, we will walk in God's overflowing blessings.

I remember when God told me that it was time to go back to school full time to pursue my doctorate. I was excited about the transition and the opportunity, but a little less thrilled to give up my full-time income. I had been accepted and had assumed that I would be given a scholarship from the graduate school. I remember the day that they told me that my acceptance did not include financial support. I told the Lord, I have already given my job notice of my leave, if this is your will you are going to have to open the door. The same time this occurred, I was scheduled to have surgery on my foot and would not be able to work or even walk. I remember feeling so helpless, but when we are weak God has the opportunity to be strong. I continued to sow, not knowing where my next check would come from. The day I was deciding whether to take a teaching position at another university, the graduate school I was planning to attend called me and offered me a teaching stipend. I also received an additional fellowship that provides financial support while you are pursuing graduate school full-time. Though I had to walk away from everything, it was during this time I saw how God may not come when I wanted Him to, but He will be there right on time. Even after I began school, it was still challenging living on a much smaller income, but when we don't have enough to meet the need, it's time to sow a seed. Every time I sowed, God would continually supply for all of my needs. I praise God that during that time not one bill went unpaid. When you are a single parent or individual, you sometimes feel that everything is on you, but we are truly able to see how God is faithful to provide when we give Him our all. Not only are we blessed, but we are storing up blessings for future generations.

One of my single sisters in the ministry shared with me how she came out of college and started her own business. Her business became very lucrative and the business deals continued to come. After a few years, she began to feel that God was calling her in a different direction. To the natural mind it would seem crazy to walk away from a lucrative business, with no real reason, but only with an unction from God. She shared with me how God began to reveal that He was not getting the glory in her life. She took pride in building her business and in its success. For the next few years God would begin to teach her how to trust in Him as her provider. To know that He is the one that has given her the ability to get wealth. She is amazed how each month God continually provides for her needs. As she now works for God in another area of business, he will receive all the glory in her success.

Those who sow in tears shall reap in joy.[62]

A Living Sacrifice

We are to present our bodies as a living sacrifice before God. Paul reminds that in all we do even in our eating and drinking, it should honor God. We have to ask God are we honoring His temple in our bodies. Are we eating the foods we need to eat, to do the work He has called us to do? Are we taking time to exercise? Are we getting enough rest? I know it can seem like there are not enough hours in the day, to have time to take care of ourselves. Do we want to make time to be in the hospital? Do we want to be too tired to play with our children, grandchildren, nieces, or nephews? If we are giving our bodies to God as a living sacrifice, it really shouldn't be about what we want or feel like doing? That's why it's a sacrifice. It is a sacrifice to get up early and workout; it's a labor of love to cook and not eat out all the time; and it is a sacrifice to turn off your favorite television show and just get some rest. However, the blessing is that we will have more energy, more joy, more peace, and more life to live for God's glory.

Do not be deceived, God is not mocked; for whatever a man sows, that he will also reap. For he who sows to his flesh will of the flesh reap corruption, but he who sows to the Spirit will of the Spirit reap everlasting life. And let us not grow weary while doing good, for in due season we shall reap if we do not lose heart.[63]

We have to be intentional about being a good steward of everything that God has given us. Our time, our body, our finances, our relationships, all should honor God. However, if we really do not have a plan that will keep track of our stewardship, we may find that there are areas of wasted time, resources, and energy. If we know we need to get more rest, we have to make sure that we actually get to bed by a certain time, or in order to workout, we may need to get up a little earlier. We may have to seek out additional help. Perhaps having a workout partner, joining a gym, or having a personal trainer may help you to meet your physical goals. I know that working out with someone else will always push you beyond your comfort zone. It may be other areas, like spending, where more discipline or planning is required. I remember my financial planner telling me to write down everything I spent for three months. You would be amazed at how little things can add up. It also made me accountable to discuss my finances with someone else. When you have clear goals for which you can be held accountable, it makes it more difficult to go on careless shopping sprees. You are more disciplined when you know that you are going to have to explain how you are reducing your debt or saving more money with someone else. I know women who hide their shopping sprees from their husbands. One of the most frequent single causes of divorce is financial problems. We have to learn to be accountable and trustworthy with our spending first to honor God and then it will be easier to submit to others. I think of the parable of the talents. Jesus explained how all the men were given a particular amount of talents according to what they had the ability to manage. One had been given five and invested and brought back five more, one had been given two and returned with two more. Their master commended the faithful stewards.

THE ONE

His lord said to him, 'Well done, good and faithful servant; you have been faithful over a few things, I will make you ruler over many things. Enter into the joy of your lord.'[64]

There are blessings, peace and joy that comes from being faithful to what God has given us to manage. However, to the one steward who had been given one and hid it in the ground, his master was so displeased that he had not invested it, at the very least, he could have put it in the bank and gained interest. He was required to give the one talent he had to the servant with ten talents. If he had only been faithful with his one talent, he would have been rewarded just as the servant with five talents. All he could focus on was his lack and the fear of losing his one talent, but it is impossible to please God without faith. Whether God has given us little or much, we have to give it back to Him to increase. If you realize that you have been given much, than much more is required. I think of all the shows where people risk everything with the possibility of winning a million dollars. We have been given a guarantee to walk in the blessings of the One who owns everything, yet we bury our talents in the ground. When we are faithful even with little, God says that He will make us ruler over many things. We have to start with being faithful in where we are now, our homes, our jobs, our family, in order to be able to receive greater blessings.

Jaquetta Williams, a minister and marriage counselor, shared with me some key lessons all single women must understand before entering into a relationship. She explained how it is important to learn how to submit to the word of God during your singleness, in order to be able to respect your husband's word in marriage. If you are able to submit to God, when He says "No, you can't have that right now" it will not be a major issue in your relationship. She also recommended how important it is to be able to operate in discipline and self-control when things don't go your way. If you are quick to get an attitude or you haven't learned to control your temper, it will cause major problems in all your relationships. Lastly, she pointed out how many women she has counseled who thought they were ready for marriage but really had more work to do in submitting their lives completely to God. She shared how she is so grateful that God allowed her to marry later, when she was spiritually ready to receive all that He had in store for her. She explained how God wants wives to be a good steward to His sons, He doesn't want them in relationships that will deter His will in their lives either. All of our relationships must be led by God: our work relationships, our ministry relationships, our relationships with our husbands and kids should all be based on the word of God.

We must be willing to submit every area of our lives to God, knowing that He only wants His best for us. God has a time and a season for every blessing. There are things we have prayed for, but we must be willing to wait on God's perfect timing. I remember growing up in California and having a peach tree in our yard. That tree produced some of the sweetest, juiciest peaches you could ever imagine. They were perfect for peach cobbler or just by themselves. It seems like it would take forever for them to ripen to sweet perfection. I remember in my haste picking one too early and being bitterly disappointed and unsatisfied. That is exactly how we will feel when we try to manipulate situations in impatience. God promises that His blessings do not come with sorrow. We bring sorrow and bitterness upon ourselves when we try to move ahead when God says not now. We can never satisfy ourselves the way God will because He knows what we need more than we do. Can you think of times when there was something you just knew you couldn't live without and then when you were able to have it, you didn't really want it anymore? Be grateful for times when God says no, because then you know He has something better in store. I am so grateful for the relationships God ended in my life that would have only led me away from His perfect will for my life. I am thankful for jobs he denied me that would have thrown me off course or blessings that would have kept me from seeking Him as my ultimate source. At the time it may be painful; you may feel rejected, but that is the time to rejoice because something greater is in store.

Lonely Lauri can spend the rest of her life mourning the marriage that never happened or she can celebrate that God had to supernaturally intervene in order to prevent her from making a huge mistake. Lauri can now see how she had put Troy in a place that only God should hold. Troy had become her everything and went she lost him, she felt like she had lost everything. However, it was actually then that she began to gain everything. She gained a deeper relationship with her first love, a greater self-esteem, a new outlook on life. Instead of being bitter, she is determined to be better. Lauri could now see how blinded she was to all the signs that Troy was not the one. Slowly she is allowing God to heal her broken heart and restore the joy she once had; a joy that will not be dependent on other people, but on her love for God. God is the ONE who had continued to love her unconditionally, even when she did not deserve such amazing love, the ONE who was always there, the ONE who never left her alone.

Prayer

Lord, forgive me for not giving you my very best in all areas of my life. You have given me your very best. You gave your only son to die for my sins, let me live my life in honor of the sacrifice you made for me. Help me to honor you in every decision I make. Show me how I can be a better steward of everything that you have given to me. Lord, everything that I have is because of your grace. Let me not give more attention to the blessings, than the ONE who has provided every blessing. Lord, I present my body as a living sacrifice, holy and acceptable which is only reasonable when I think of all that you have given me. Lord, you will be glorified in my life.

THE ONE

Chapter Six
Letting Go, Letting God

For peace of mind...resign as general manager of the universe.[65]

I remember being a young girl listening to "Control" by Janet Jackson and singing it with such conviction. "I want to be the one in control!" I feel that my generation and the younger generation of women have been raised with an independence and sense of ownership that our mother's generation did not embrace whole-heartedly. I do believe in the importance of being able to have rights and privileges that were once denied to women. There is nothing wrong with being a successful businesswoman or leader in your community. However, I do believe that sometimes our need for control can disable us from walking by faith, with a total dependence upon God. It may also create friction within our marriages. We all quote, the phrase "Let go and let God," but do we truly let go and allow God to have His way? We say not my will but yours be done, but really want His will to be our will. It is so important that we truly learn to allow God to reign in our lives. He opens doors we would have never been able to open on our own. God tells us that He loads us with daily benefits. How sad would it be to miss out on the blessings God has prepared for us each day because we are so committed to our own agenda. Yes, we must make plans and set goals, but it is vital that we seek God's direction in this process so that our goals are in alignment with His will for our lives.

For whoever desires to save his life will lose it, but whoever loses his life for My sake will find it.[66]

We have to be willing to let go, in order to receive. I was helping my mother do some spring cleaning and, though my mother's home is always immaculate, we were amazed by the amount of clothes, papers, and other odds and ends that had accumulated in closets and other areas hidden beyond view. If you have ever moved, you can understand how things can easily accumulate. Many times, you find things that you forgot you had. I have heard organizers suggest that you shouldn't buy anything new until you let go of something old. One thing I have found is that as you begin to organize, you end up finding things you thought you had needed, tucked away in the back of a closet somewhere. I think there are areas spiritually where we think we are lacking and fail to realize that God has already given us everything we need. Many times our lives may appear picture perfect to others, but we must be willing to allow God to clean the areas that are hidden from public view; memories, pain, and emotional strongholds that can keep our lives filled with unnecessary clutter.

One of my single sisters shared with me how clutter in her home often reflects clutter in her mind and spirit. Have you ever been to someone's house and could barely sit down because of all the clutter, or do you find your living space cluttered with knick knacks and papers that you just can't seem to get rid of? I can remember watching television program that show the effects of becoming a hoarder and not being able to let go of anything. When seeing the extreme cases where people cannot invite people over or even move around in their own homes because of such a great accumulation of things, you wonder how it can get that bad. Often times their natural or physical state reflects a much deeper spiritual problem, primarily based in fear; a fear that they will lack if they give this item away or that they may need it in the future. However, when they had personal organizers come in and remove loads and loads of items they really did not need, they were so relieved and excited to now be able to invite their family and friends back into their lives. They now had control over their things and their possessions no longer possessed them. They were grateful for the help they received in reclaiming their lives. Sometimes, we are going to have to get help from others. I have one friend who is a professional organizer and helped me to organize the layout of my home office. Another one of my friends is just naturally gifted in administration and is truly a blessing in my life. First, we must be willing to admit that this may not be our strongest area so I need help. When we are weak, God is strong and He will send people in our lives to help us become all that we need to be in Him.

Give, and it shall be given unto you; good measure, pressed down, and shaken together, and running over, shall men give into your bosom.[67]

Many times we are only holding on to the past out of fear that we will not be able to replace the things we need to leave behind. I recently moved and there were few things God allowed me to bring with me. At first, I had planned to sell them and then God told me to give away my new furniture and clothes. I had only had the furniture for a year, but I realized that it was never meant for me to keep it, but to give it to bless someone else's life. Some of the things we may have to give up may seem very valuable in our eyes and in the eyes of others, but we have to know that God has something much more valuable to give to us. God gives the gift of peace, to know that we never have to worry about our needs being unmet and with the same measure that we give it will be given back to us. It never comes in the way we think it will come, but we are always blessed as we bless others. I remember one year cleaning out my closet and getting rid of anything that did not reflect the person God was molding me into. I had things from high school and college that didn't reflect who I had become in Christ. God was preparing me to be a successful woman and many of the clothes I gave away reminded me of my life as a student. After giving away the clothes, that same week I went to visit my older cousin. My cousin was once a model, and always dressed with impeccable grace and style. While I was at her house, she literally gave me a trunk full of clothes, some with the tags still attached! I learned a valuable lesson that week. God wants to bless us with more, but we have to be willing to let go of the old. Many times we think we are cursed not blessed when we are stripped of everything we hold to be valuable. However, it does not necessarily mean that God is punishing us, but that He wants His glory to be shown even brighter in our lives.

I think of how because of Job's righteousness, God knew He would be glorified even as he was stripped of everything that was dear to him; his possessions, his family, his health, yet He still remained faithful to God stating,

"The Lord gave, and the Lord has taken away; Blessed be the name of the Lord."[68] Job understood an important truth, that everything he had was a gift from God. I think it is often difficult to give something to God when we think it is something that we have attained on our own; this is my job, my business, my money, or my child. However, every good and perfect gift comes from God. Job was extremely prosperous, but he never allowed his possessions to possess him. He was grateful to have them, but he would still bless the Lord without them. Despite the rejection and ridicule Job faced "he did not sin nor charge God with wrong."[69] Even his wife told Job to curse God and die, but he asked her how can we accept blessings from God and not be willing to accept adversity. This is truly an awesome man of God. We all want the blessings, but not trials or tests that may come with that blessing. We look at other people and think how nice it would be to live like they live, but we never know the depth of the sacrifice they have had to make to attain that blessing. It may not be as appealing if we knew what we would have to endure for that level of blessing.

Job's closest friends tried to make him feel as though it were his fault, but God told Job to pray for them and after that God restored all that he lost. Many of us will not be restored until we are able to forgive those who have wrongfully accused us and made us feel less than what we know God has called us to be. We cannot allow their ignorance to block our blessing. Jesus was able to ask the Father to "forgive them for they know not what they do." We can't hold it against them because they are only doing what they know to do. Though Job lost everything, because of his faithfulness he not only received back all that he lost, but twice as much was given to him. He also was stronger in his faith and trust in God. Even if he didn't receive it all back, he knew how to bless God at all times, regardless of the circumstances or trials he had to face. Many times God has to strip us of everything so that we can receive his full blessings and not allow the blessings to take God's place in our life.

You can clutch the past so tightly to your chest that it leaves your arms too full to embrace the present.
Jan Glidewell

I am reminded of my sister in Christ who has such a tremendous testimony of how God stripped her of everything in order to bring her into a new level of glory in Him. She always knew God had a call on her life, but it was revealed even more through the trials she has had to endure throughout her life. After suffering the loss of her fiancé, she decided that it was time for a new start in a new city. She and her sons had to start from scratch after paying someone to help her move and having him steal everything they owned. She was working three jobs to make ends meet, when she was dealt another difficult blow. She had only been in Atlanta for three months when she suffered a massive stroke that left her in a coma for weeks. She said she could remember laying there unable to speak or move, but she could hear the voices of the doctors and family members in the room. She literally heard them planning her funeral right over her. Being overwhelmed with frustration and sadness, she began to well up with tears which let them know that she was responsive. Once she came out of the coma, the doctors only gave her a week to live. Her brain and all her major organs were beginning to shut down; her body was convulsing in seizures every hour. She did not want to live her life like that and began to contemplate suicide. When her children were finally allowed to see her, it was her eight-year-old son who prayed over her and gave her strength to fight for her life. She told the Lord she didn't care if she remained in that state as long as He would receive the glory from her life. Once she surrendered to God's will, her miraculous recovery astounded the doctors.

After being confined to a wheel chair, God miraculously healed her during a conference and gave her back the mobility of the side that had been stricken by the stroke. Today her testimony continues to give God glory and encourages others to break free from spiritual, physical, and emotional bondage. She shared with me the awesome joy and love she has for God. When I asked her what advice she would give to other single women, she shared how it is important for single women to go back to being God's bride and to seek Him for their covering. One has to be God's bride first in order to be prepared to be someone else's bride. Lastly, she shared how we must seek for God to increase as we decrease. She could have allowed the past to dictate her future, but she believed that God had not forgotten her and would give her a brighter future.

I like how Paul stated I may not know much, but one thing I must do is to forget all the things in my past in order to reach forward and press toward a higher calling in Christ Jesus.[70] We will never be able to forget the pain of the past when we are always looking back. In order to move forward we must continually look forward and press our way through every obstacle. It is also difficult to move forward when we are weighted down by emotional baggage of bitterness, envy, anger, or other sins. Thankfully, Jesus tells us to come to Him when we feel burdened, stressed, and heavy laden and He will give us rest. It was never God's will for us to carry the burdens we do, but it is up to us to let them go. Once we surrender our cares to Him, we will find that His yoke is easy and His burden is light. God promises to never give us more than we can bear, but we often place demands on ourselves that are unreasonable. We must stop and ask ourselves, is this God will for me to take on this burden or am I trying to prove something to myself or others? It sometimes feels like there are not enough hours in the day, but if we begin to allow God to be our first priority He knows how much time we need to complete what He has given us to do. We have to learn to go with the flow and trust Him to lead us. We feel we should already be at a certain point in our lives and compare ourselves to others, but we must be confident that God is completing the work He has begun in us. It is not according to our timetable, but to his divine schedule. So we are reminded to not be anxious about anything, but to present our requests with thanksgiving, knowing He is working everything out for our good.

Do not remember the former things, nor consider the things of old. Behold, I will do a new thing, Now it shall spring forth; Shall you not know it?[71]

We miss out on tremendous opportunities, experiences, or relationships when we are constantly focusing on negative aspects of past experiences or relationships. Though my father flew on planes in the military, he had a tremendous fear of flying. When he was younger a plane crashed near his house and the fear of crashing in a plane stayed with him. Though we drove all over the country for vacations, he would never fly. Through her job, my mother had the opportunity to go to Hawaii and other beautiful places, but my father would never go with her because of his fear. What fear are you holding on to that is keeping you from enjoying new experiences or relationships? It may seem very logical and justified in your mind, but the root is based in fear and not in faith. We will not see that God is doing a new thing if we are constantly focused on the past. It is possible that new things are springing forth and we are in a new place and yet we don't even know it. Many women condemn themselves with guilt and pain from past mistakes, not realizing that once they asked God for forgiveness, He no longer remembers their sin. Women who come out of abusive or destructive relationships think that this kind of relationship is the best they can do and really don't look for much more. The minute we realize who we are as children of the Most High God and how much He loves us, we can begin to expect Him to do great things in our lives. Not because we are so worthy, but because of His awesome love for us.

When you do break away from old relationships, it may not only be material possessions that you need to leave, but also alliances and habits that are not allowing you to move to a new place in God. Too Through Tina and Lonely Lauri must be able to release the ugliness of their past relationships in order to receive beautiful relationships in the future. They are actually allowing the people that hurt them to keep them in bondage. While they are free to live their lives, they are reliving the pain day after day. Though they may feel justified in holding on to the hurt and pain, by doing so they are aborting the birth of a new more confident and loving woman in Christ. They may have to pray and fast to seek God to be released from soul ties and destructive emotional habits that continue to keep them in bondage.

Tina and Lauri have already been given victory in Christ, but they must claim it in their lives. We must allow old things to pass away, before all things can become new. The only way we can do that is to give them to Christ and allow Him to cleanse us and purify our hearts. He will give us a new song to sing. A song of praise and not of despair, but we must want to sing a new song. People can actually become comfortable in seeing themselves as the perpetual victim and having others show them pity for things that happened years and years ago. We have to be willing to take a step out of the place of pain into a place of praise. The more we focus on all the blessings we have been given and God's unconditional love, the easier it will be to receive His joy and peace in our lives.

God's To –Do List

In order to truly let go and let God, we have to realize what we can handle and what we have to give to God. I encourage you to make a list of what you need to do and what you are giving to God. On my To-Do list I know I must seek Him daily and trust Him to guide my path. I have to prepare myself for the opportunities, relationships, and responsibilities He is giving me. I must daily walk in faith to recognize those opportunities and boldly claim them for His glory. It is God's responsibility to provide for me. He promised me that He is my shepherd and I do not have to be in want. He promised to give me a hope and a future. He promised that He would never leave or forsake me and that He would send His Holy Spirit as a comforter. He will place the opportunities, relationships, and blessings in our path as long as we follow His lead. Really, when you begin to look at it God has much more to do concerning you than you do. We just have to be obedient to His will.

THE ONE

The Lord will perfect that which concerns me.[72]

Isn't it wonderful to know that God is working out His perfect plan in every area that concerns you. When I want to throw up my hands, I can read this verse and know that God's got it. I don't have to stress or worry about anything; He already is perfecting that which concerns me. If we really are doing our part in trusting God, why are we worrying? Jesus cannot understand why we would worry about the daily concerns of life. Think of all the times you were planning for a big event stressing about what you were going to wear? Jesus tells us just us to look at the lilies and how even Solomon was not clothed with such splendor. If God even cares about the lilies, how much more concerned is He about fulfilling His plan in your life. All these concerns and worries take our focus off of God, which should be our number one concern. Jesus reminds us not to worry about tomorrow; just seek God and His righteousness and all these things will be added to us.

Prayer

Lord, I thank you for giving me a hope and a future. Today, I am letting go of the pain of rejection, abuse, and betrayal. I thank you that once You set me free I am free indeed. I no longer have to look back at the past. I can look forward to the awesome future I have in You. Lord, forgive me for all the times I doubted Your word over my life. I know that every word You have spoken must come to pass. Give me the strength and the patience to wait on Your perfect timing. I trust You to perfect that which concerns me. I can see that You are doing a new thing in my life. I don't have to try to manipulate situations for my favor; I already am favored by You. You will do exceedingly, abundantly more than I could ever ask or think. Amen.

Chapter Seven
Fit For the King

He has made everything beautiful in its time.[74]

If you asked single women if they were ready to be married, many would say "Yes" enthusiastically. However if you asked those same women, would they be willing to leave their families by force, forget about everything they had planned for the next year, and move in with complete strangers, many would be much more hesitant in their response. This is only part of what Esther had to endure in order to become queen of Persia. After losing both her parents and being raised by her cousin, Mordecai, she was forced to leave the only safe place she had known. She was not given a choice about whether or not she wanted to go. We never think about the plans Esther may have had prior to being taken to the king's palace. At the time, it must have been extremely hard to leave the only remaining family she had left. It shows how Esther learned to be obedient to the will of God and submit to those in authority. As single women, we must realize that as great as our plans may be, God has even greater plans for our lives. His plans are more than we could have even thought or dreamt to be possible, but we must be willing to die to ourselves in order to be prepared for the greater work He has in store.

Esther was told by Mordecai, not to reveal her Jewish identity, and she obeyed his instructions. Esther, whose name was Hadassah, meant "star" in Hebrew. She was created to shine and she shined with humility and grace. She immediately found favor with the king's servant Hegai. He gave her the best living quarters and the best maidservants. Even in the midst of God, seemingly stripping us of everything, He gives us favor and provision. Esther would have to go through a twelve-month process of purification. The women were required to go through six months with oil of myrrh and six months with sweet spices and perfumes and other purification processes. The herbs and spices they used to anoint them not only provided aromatherapy, but also healing benefits. Myrrh is still commonly used in perfumes to this day. However, in ancient times it was very valuable at one time being worth more than its weight in gold. Myrrh was used in incense and perfume; it also was beneficial in stimulating blood flow, reducing pain, and improving skin conditions. Esther was being prepared to walk in royalty, but first she would have to release the pain and hurt she felt physically, emotionally, and spiritually. God loves us enough to give us the most valuable preparation in order to walk in his promise.

When the time came for Esther to go before the king, she only took what Hegai, the king's attendant recommended. She learned how to submit her will to someone else in order for her to be her best. This shows how she realized that Hegai, would know how what the king would desire more than she would. God will put people in our lives to prepare us to walk in favor, but we must be willing to learn how to please our great King. First, we must go through a purification process to remove impurities and flaws in our character. We may have to leave some things behind that we would have desired, but is not what our King would require. When king Ahaserus saw Esther, she immediately found favor in his sight. The royal crown was placed upon her head and a holiday was declared in her honor. It may have appeared as if Esther had easily stepped into this position of favor overnight, but there was a much longer process that had to take place first. God wants us to learn to trust Him, to lead us into his perfect will. Regardless, of the circumstances or situation, we must trust in the word He has spoken over our lives.

Though Esther was appointed queen, she still did not reveal her Jewish heritage, until Mordecai revealed that the time was right. When she learned of the plot to kill all people of Jewish ancestry for serving God and not worshipping the King by bowing in his presence, she still could not go to see her cousin Mordecai. But her messenger sent her word from him of all that was plotted against her people by Haman. Esther fasted and requested her people fast as well, knowing that if she approached the King without being called, she could be killed. Mordecai encouraged her to know that she had been sent "for such a time as this."[75] God appointed Esther, because He knew she would obey Him and still keep Him in first place in her life. She could have been denounced as queen, but God gave her favor with the king. The reason she was chosen to be queen was greater than her destiny alone; she would be in a position to affect the destiny of future generations far beyond her.

She honored her husband by preparing a great feast for him for two days. What an example of a virtuous woman who does not come to her husband bickering and complaining about what he must do. She could have complained about why he had not requested her presence in over a month. Yet, she honored her king and delighted in him. She must have prepared a spectacular feast because the king was so pleased that he told her whatever she wanted he would give it to her, even half the kingdom. She blessed him and Haman, who had ordered the decree, and on the second day and gracefully made her request for her people. How Esther was able to withstand being in the presence of Haman, knowing what he had planned against her people, showed her grace. But God even tells us to bless our enemies, knowing that vengeance will be from the Lord. On the same day, Haman had plotted to hang her cousin Mordecai, and the enemy put it on the heart of the king to bless Mordecai for saving his life. It shows us how if we are patient, God will make our enemies our footstool. When the king discovered what Haman had plotted, he was hanged, instead of Mordecai and the decree against her people was revoked. Mordecai and Esther were both exalted in the king's palace and their people were honored.

As we examine the story of Esther, we learn that as we seek The One, He will lead us to the right one to complete the great work He has given us to do. The people God puts us in relationship with are to accomplish a greater work that will bring Him glory. We must learn that it is not about us. Though God wants His best for us, He also wants us to keep Him first in our heart. As we submit to His will, we may feel as though He is breaking us, but it is only so He can exalt us to a higher place in Him. Even through the trials, we must continue to give God praise.

THE ONE

<u>Praise to the King</u>

Enter into His gates with thanksgiving,
And into His courts with praise.
Be thankful to Him, and bless His name.[76]

How many times do we enter into God's presence solely to give Him praise? How many times do we come to God in fear and dump all of our problems on Him like a dump truck. We feel better, but is this what God desires from us? He tells us to come into His presence with praise on our lips. When we come to Him in fear, it shows how we really don't trust Him to do what He promised he would do in our lives. I think of the disciples waking Jesus in the storm to ask Him to do something. He asks them why are they fearful and says that it reveals their lack of faith. Though they had walked at Jesus' side and seen His miracles firsthand, they still were overcome by the circumstances of their situation. It is easy to become overwhelmed and fearful when we take our eyes off of God and focus on what appears to be a catastrophe. However, when we are continually mindful of all the wonderful things God does for us, without us even asking, it is easy to give Him praise. When we think of where we would be without His grace and mercy, we must enter His gates with thanksgiving. Regardless of what obstacles we may have to overcome, we can praise Him for being our Savior. He is the only one we can expect to be our savior.

Many times women look to men or their husbands to save them from trials, financial issues, but we must know that God is truly the source of every good thing. Yes, a good man should want to take care of his wife, but a virtuous woman does not have to pressure or nag her husband to do so, knowing her help is ultimately from the Lord. I have so many awesome women of God that I have seen support and stand by their husbands in times of plenty and in times of lack. I have known women who remained strong as their husbands left very lucrative careers to start their own business or to go into the ministry. Because of their relationship with God they were able to praise and support their husbands in what may have appeared as very dismal circumstances, but they are now reaping the benefits as their husbands prosper in God's will. Other women probably wished they had seen the potential in them earlier. Some women drive their husbands away with their lack of faith in God and in them. Solomon tells his son that there is nothing worse than a nagging woman. Solomon reveals in Proverbs that death and life are in the power of the tongue. Women have the power to speak life or death into our relationships. In the very next line of Proverbs, Solomon states, "He who finds a wife finds a good thing."[77] Bishop T.D. Jakes makes the following comments about this verse:

Unless you are healed and whole, your man will not feel that He's enjoying the Lord's favor in his relationship with you. Ladies, men do not exist to bring the favor of the Lord to your lives, either. You find the favor of the Lord by being the woman He created you to be – by breaking the chains with which the devil had you bound, by knowing the Lord passionately and intimately, by walking in His power and worshiping Him with your life.[78]

I truly believe that it is through our worship that anyone connected to us will receive favor, particularly our husbands. Dr. Gloria Morrow confirms that as single women we must address areas where we need to be healed, before entering into a relationship. Dr. Morrow is a licensed psychologist as well as a pastor. The first time I heard her speak was at a singles' conference at my church and she provided clarity and direction for all those who attended. I recently interviewed her to ask her advice for single women. She explained that while you are single,you have the ability to look at yourself critically and become more disciplined in various areas. In her book Keeping it Real she gives readers " 7 steps toward a healthier you." Dr. Morrow explains that one of the major problems for single women is that they are living in denial about how they are living lives of despair. You have to recognize when something is not right and begin taking steps to becoming healthy. If there is healing that needs to occur from past relationships, it must be addressed before entering into a new relationship. She states how it is important to "Deal with your emotional baggage." When you are unhealthy, you will only attract unhealthy people. However, when you are emotionally healthy, you will feel good about yourself and love who you are and attract people that also love you for who you are. Dr. Morrow explains that there is a reason for every season and while we are single we should clearly identify what our spiritual gifts are. We should develop an authentic spiritual life, by not just going to church but by actively engaging in prayer, praise, and fasting on a consistent basis. The strength of our relationship with God will prepare us to trust God in marriage and other areas of our life. Dr. Morrow admits that it was a struggle for her to go from independence to interdependence in marriage. After being single for several years and raising her son single-handedly, it was a shock when her husband told her he didn't want her to work. Though she didn't understand it at first, she knew that God honors obedience. When she left work, she was then able to go back to school full-time and eventually complete her doctorate. Dr. Morrow knows that her obedience then helped to establish her and prepare her for the ministry she has today. As we surrender our will to God, He will exalt us to an even greater level in Him.

Esther was exalted as she humbled herself as queen. As Esther worshipped her God, her children, her family, and her people were given favor. In order to become the good thing God has called us to be, we must first learn to completely trust God with our lives and then we can learn to trust God to complete the work He has for the people He has placed in our lives. I was listening to a secular writer explain how men enjoy being with women who are confident and happy. When we lose faith, we lose our joy and our confidence that God has already taken care of the situation. Through faith we can speak life into our husbands, our children, and our people. I believe that we walk in favor not just when we are married, but everyday as a woman of God. We should bring favor on our jobs, in our church, in our communities and, wherever we go, people should be blessed by our presence. Because wherever we go, the presence of the Lord goes with us.

We have to enjoy our lives. When we walk in the gifting God has given us, it naturally brings us joy. Every day is a gift from God. I want to live the abundant life God has promised to give me in Him. As women, we sometimes feel guilty about taking care of ourselves and doing the things we enjoy doing. One of the things I enjoy doing is going to the spa or just getting a massage. I had been putting it off and thinking of so many other things I needed to do. One day, I was in car accident that could have easily been fatal. After the accident, I had continuous pain in my neck and back. The pain forced me to see a chiropractor who also recommended massage therapy. My massage therapist was truly a blessing to me both physically and spiritually. I asked her what made her go into message therapy. She shared with me how her husband had been in a near fatal accident that left him paralyzed. She learned massage therapy to minister to her husband. She continues to believe God for his complete recovery. She has shared with me so many lessons about what a covenant relationship entails and how important it is to put your trust in the Lord. She shared that as a single person, God has you completely to himself, mind, soul, and body. When you're married, your body is not your own. You can't just go on a fast and not consult your husband. When you are single, you have the freedom to give yourself completely to God. There are so many spiritual nuggets and secrets God can share with us when He has our total devotion. I know it was God's will to bring this special lady into my life. I didn't realize how my accident would work for my good in the end. I know as she is helping to heal me physically as I am also growing spiritually. I think about how Esther also received aromatherapy and spa treatments to be prepared for her king. God will prepare us for what He has planned for us. Though the process may be painful at times, if we endure to the end, we will receive a great reward. We have to continue to give Him praise even as we are being prepared for the promise.

I waited patiently for the Lord; and He inclined to me and heard my cry.[79]

Many times it seems as if God has not heard our cry, but He has. I am sure Esther wondered when her turn would come to go to the King. Perhaps she was one of the last ladies to be called. The word tells us to be anxious for nothing, but with thanksgiving to let our requests be made known to God and He will give us peace that surpasses all understanding.[80] We have to continue to give God praise even as we wait for our king. There will always be something that we must believe God for, it may not be marriage, but your business, your children, relief from financial debt, physical healing, or perhaps all of the above. We must remember that God knows our needs before we even know we have a need. God has already provided for every need we will ever have, but we must trust God as we wait on His perfect timing. I know there have been many times when I felt I needed something now, but if I had received it when I wanted to receive it, I would not have been ready for it. Good parents know they cannot give their children everything they want, but they do plan to meet their needs at a specific time. How much more will our Father give us good gifts at the appropriate time? We must wait on God with praise in our hearts, knowing that He will supply everything we need. Many think of waiting as such a passive thing to do, but if you have ever observed a waiters or waitresses they have very busy jobs. They are wholly concerned with meeting the needs of others and when they do their jobs well, they are tipped well. When we are concerned with meeting the needs of our Great King, He will surely reward us for our diligence. Our focus should not be on what we need, but on what He needs from us, and He will make sure our need is supplied.

Prayer

Lord, I thank you for being patient with me, even when I haven't been patient. I surrender my will to Your will for my life. I thank you for preparing me now to walk in greatness. Though sometimes the process is painful, I know that the suffering of this present time is nothing, when compared to the glory that will be revealed in me. I thank you for allowing me to be a blessing to everyone around me. As I set my heart toward pleasing you, you will make sure that I have everything I need. I thank you that I will be healed and whole in you. Thank you for orchestrating the situations in my life that I walk in favor in every area of my life. I will continue to trust You to complete the good work You have begun in me.

THE ONE

Chapter Eight
Pursuing Passion: A Single Purpose

Now, more than ever, is the time when we should pursue our passion. As we take the time to seek God for our purpose, we will be lead to the opportunities and relationships that will help us to complete His plan for our lives. Sometimes God will redirect our plans to fulfill a greater purpose for our lives. From the time I was a little girl, I said that I wanted to become a lawyer. So when I went to college, I majored in Political Science and Communication. My junior year I had the opportunity to do an internship with the Department of Justice. I loved working in the press office and helping with speeches, but the courtroom was not as glamorous, nor as exciting as I had viewed it in my mind. I only had one more year and I began to seriously doubt my career choice. Luckily, I doubled majored in communication and loved assisting students with their speeches and communication skills. My professor recommended that I apply to graduate school in communication, which I had not thought about before. I did apply to graduate school, which eventually brought me to Georgia. I had no friends or family in

Georgia, but now I can see how it was clearly in God's plan for me to be here. However, God's plan for my life was not always so clear. Even after graduating with my Master of Arts, I had doubts about what I wanted to do. It was during that time that I truly began to seek God for purpose and direction.

One day I started writing about an experience that I had had and it eventually turned into my first book, Changing Lanes: A New Adult's Guide to Understanding Your Lane in Life. I had no plans of being an author although I had always used writing to express myself, even as a child. Writing had always been therapeutic for me as I went through difficult times. As a child and young adult, I always tutored other children and enjoyed speaking and teaching others new things. I began to understand my God-given gifts, by realizing what came naturally to me. I have always enjoyed teaching, writing, and empowering others to do their best. Then I realized that everything I do must relate to those core gifts. As a professor, author, talk show host, and communication consultant, I am able to use all of those gifts in different ways. I know there are things that you do without even thinking about it. There are things that come naturally to you that do not come naturally to others. There are several books that can help you in discovering your key gifts and allow you to begin writing a mission plan for your life. I mentioned Dr. Gloria Morrow, who has books in this area. I have also benefitted from several books by Valorie Burton, a nationally known author, life-coach, and speaker. She was one of the people who motivated me to publish my first book. For this book, she graciously shared some suggestions for single women in discovering their purpose.

I asked Valorie how she discovered her purpose. She shared how she had an epiphany in 1999 when she was in a bookstore. She began to realize that ever since she was a child, she had always been passionate about books. Valorie explained how many times in life we get into a routine and forget the things that make us who we are. We have to take ourselves back to our childhood, when we didn't have worries, and re-discover our passion and the things that bring us joy. She shared how even as a single women, we can be extremely busy. We must take the time to take care of ourselves and make room for the things that bring us joy. Valorie shared how, "Being busy is not the same as being significant." We must realize how everything we do should help us to fulfill our purpose. There may be activities that you have to drop and people you have to say no to, in order to make room for you to pursue your top priorities. First, we have to know what is truly important to us and then we can be intentional about how we spend our time. What priorities are non-negotiable? We have to take care of our spiritual and physical well-being. We also have to make the time to spend with friends, family, and doing things that are fun. Valorie shared how single women should not delay things until they get married. If you desire to travel or buy a house, you should pursue those goals. When she reconnected with her now husband, she had successfully established herself as an author and life-coach. She remembers telling God that though she desired to be married, she was at peace with not getting married. She had learned to be content in all the things God had called her to do. Shortly, after surrendering her will to God, she received a call from the man who is now her husband. She shared the importance of not worrying about "who" will be the one, but rather living in the moment and pursuing your purpose.

Being Honest with Yourself

The first step to any authentic relationship comes from knowing who you are. We can never be honest with others if we are not honest with ourselves. Many times when people don't take the time to truly discover what matters most to them, they are continually seeking to please others. People-pleasing will continue to manifest in family relationships, dating relationships, friendships, work relationships, and in marriage. However, maintaining the façade can only last so long when apart of you is dying on the inside. You will eventually become angry, bitter, and frustrated with them, when it is really about you. No one will ever be good enough, supportive enough, or giving enough to meet all your needs.

I think about the character Julia Roberts played in the movie Runaway Bride. Every relationship she was in she would become what the other person and like what they liked, enjoy hobbies that they enjoyed, and do the things they liked to do. Yet, she never could commit to them in marriage because I believe deep down she knew that the relationship was based on a lie. One day she had to stop and assess who she was and what she liked to do. When she truly discovered who she was then she was able to commit her true self in an authentic relationship.

Lonely Lauri's life is similar to the Julia Roberts character, jumping from one relationship into the next. Though she was continually in a relationship, there was still a part of her that felt empty and alone. Lauri, began to realize that it wasn't her former fiancé Troy that she missed, but her feelings were rooted in not having the love of her father. She never really got over the feeling of abandonment she felt by never knowing her natural father. She felt that something must be wrong with her. Her fear of being alone would often cause her to stay in relationships that were destructive and painful. Though she was in pain in the relationship, she was only now beginning to address the true pain she felt from her childhood. She didn't want to be alone with her emotions and fears. However, now God can begin to heal her need for unconditional love that only He can give. She was trying to use people to fulfill needs that only God can meet. She now can see her value and worth through her Heavenly Father's eyes. She is beginning to enjoy spending time with herself, doing the things she is passionate about doing. Lauri now enjoys spending more quality time with her friends and has even become involved in her church's nursery. People are beginning to see the transition from Lonely Lauri to Loveable Lauri. She is loving herself more than she ever had before. She is more passionate about her relationship with God. She is loving life more and more each day.

When we are honest with ourselves, we can begin to love ourselves and love the life we have been given. We will not be afraid of being alone because we enjoy our own company. I am so grateful for the times I share with just me and God. I think many people who jump into committed relationships at an early age never truly have time to solidify who they are as individuals. Many times you hear people speak about how they grew apart. This often happens because they began to discover who they really are and what really matters to them; they realize that the person they were in a relationship with did not share their values. It is important before entering any type of relationship that we know what key values we have, it could be related to family, spiritual values, individual goals, or community involvement. I remember watching a biography on Coretta

Scott King that showed when Dr. Martin Luther King Jr. first asked her to marry him, she didn't respond right away because she knew that she was not marrying a man but a vision. However, she realized that she shared the same vision he had and often encouraged his participation in the Civil Rights Movement. She went into the marriage knowing that though she would have to sacrifice some aspects of her life, she ultimately shared the same values and passion he had for others. When we know what our vision in life is, we will begin to attract others who share that same vision. Though you are different people, you will complement one another well and be agreed on your direction and purpose. I love the verse that says, "Can two walk together, unless they are agreed?"[81] We must know who we are and what we are agreeing to, before we can truly walk with another person in any relationship. It could be a business partner, but if the other person has a completely different vision than you have for the business, you will have difficulty being on one accord. It could be reflected in your workplace. I have had to leave companies and organizations when I began to see unethical practices being portrayed as a standard part of their business. Though I don't think it was happenstance that I was there to bring light to some of the issues, eventually, I knew I had to leave. When you sacrifice your moral values in order to be a part of any relationship or organization, eventually, you will be left unfulfilled. However, when we know who we are, we can begin to walk with others who respect and support our unique calling in life.

Today I have given you the choice between life and death, between blessings and curses. Now I call on heaven and earth to witness the choice you make. Oh, that you would choose life, so that you and your descendants might live![82]

Breaking the Cycle of Pain

Dr. Cloud shares how singles should have a full life as they seek wholeness in a fulfilling relationship with Christ and others. Drs. Henry Cloud and John Townsend have great books on addressing boundaries in dating relationships, marriage, and children. In order to break cycles of pain, we have to know our own personal boundaries to know when others have crossed those boundaries. You have to clearly know what you will accept and what you will not accept. A whole woman will not allow herself to be in relationships that are destructive, hurtful, abusive, or one-sided. I love the saying that if you don't stand for something you fall for anything. If you know that your spiritual life is an authentic part of who you are, you can never truly walk in agreement with someone who does not honor that part of who you are. Many times when we are just getting to know someone, we look over many things, but we must go into any relationship with our eyes open. I love the quote by Maya Angelou, "When someone shows you who they are, believe them." If you know who you are and realize that your girlfriend, boyfriend, co-worker, family member, is not the type of person you want to be around, then you may need to limit your interaction with them. Many times people in dating relationships think that somehow by marrying a person with clearly destructive personality traits, they can shape them into the person they want. It never works and the cycle of pain often becomes worse. People are who they are and yes we all are in process, but we have to accept where people are now in order to walk with them later.

Desperate Debra, longed so desperately to be in a relationship and to be shown attention, that she would often become involved in very destructive relationships. Debra is beginning to learn to be honest with herself and to address how her childhood pain and lack of attention has created a destructive cycle of trying to use men to fill a void in her soul. Only God can truly heal her and fill her life with joy that is not based on other people's opinion of her, but rather on who she knows she is in God. As Debra begins to ask herself why she is always in dead-end relationships and address the root of the problem, she will then be able to move past the pain. Debra began to notice that the cycles of pain and divorce seem to be all around her. Most of the women in her family were not pursuing their passion and were continually in abusive or dysfunctional relationships. Debra is transforming from desperate to determined – determined that the cycle of pain and hurt will end with her. Debra is determined to show the other women in her family how to live a life of joy and peace in Christ. For years Debra simply existed, but today she is choosing to live.

Careless Carrie is also determined to end the cycle of abuse she has experienced. She now has a freedom in Christ that she never had before. Careless Carrie is now becoming more caring about her own children's futures as well as those in her community. Carrie and Debra are pursuing their passion by starting a nonprofit to support teenage girls who have come from abusive pasts. Everything that was used to bring them down, they will now use to lift up others and prevent them from entering into a destructive cycle. God has truly worked all things together for the good in their lives, and they will show their thankfulness by living each day to the fullest.

Pursuing Passion Daily

I love how the song "Golden" by Jill Scott shows how we must choose to walk in freedom. It is a conscious decision to allow joy to manifest in our lives. Regardless of the circumstances we face, we are going to sing a new song and it won't be "Whoa is me." It will be a song of praise. When we walk by faith and not by sight God is so proud of us. We know that whatever presents itself that day God's got it all under control. God just wants us to trust Him and give Him praise continually. We may not understand how it will workout, but we know He's already worked it out.

Hesitant Heather is tired of living her life half-heartedly. She is ready to step out and live the life she has dreamed about. She is going to pursue her dream of being a travel agent and is already planning a trip for her and her girlfriends to go to South Africa. She is helping Victoria make arrangements for her honeymoon. Every day she will take one more step closer to realizing her dream. One day she realized that she has more to lose by not pursuing her dream than by maintaining her mediocre existence. So now, instead of dreading to wake up in the morning, she is beginning to look forward to each new day, knowing that there are new blessings waiting to be claimed. Instead of being hesitant about every decision, she is all owing God to have His way. She may only be able to see one day at a time, but she knows that eventually she will reach her goals.

Too Through Tina, has begun to see that many of the limitations in her life had been self-created. She never thought she could go back to school or do well on her own, but she is doing well in her paralegal program. In fact, she is able to do many things she thought she could never do. She had to begin to see her life as a blessing and not a curse. As she began to expect a better life, she actually began to live a better life. Instead of dwelling on all the negative pain of Tyrone's adultery, she is able to thank God she did not lose her mind in the process. God kept her when she didn't even realize she was being kept. Things she would have normally taken on herself, she is now able to trust God to handle. Instead of Too Through Tina, she has now become Trusting Tina. She trusts God to give her a new beginning in life through His love.

Busy Brittany realized that there were so many things competing for her attention. Once she was able to allow herself to be still and to hear what God was really calling her to do, many things she thought were so important, didn't even matter. Every morning, instead of rushing out the door, she was taking time to allow God to reveal His plan for her that day. She has noticed that it is has made all the difference. Brittany always knew that as busy as she was, there was something more she needed; she found that it was a true relationship with Christ. She had always known about God, but she was not in a relationship with Him. She is more fulfilled in her relationship with Christ than any relationship or business endeavor. Her relationship with God has actually enhanced all her other relationships and business goals because not they are purposeful. She realizes now that being busy does not mean she is doing God's will. As she seeks to fulfill His will for her life, she has more time to do the things that truly help her to live the life she desires. She realizes that she has been blessed with many gifts and where much is given, much is required. She continues to trust God to complete the work He has begun in her.

Virtuous Victoria, is so grateful to see her girl-friends walking in a greater relationship with God and for their support on her special day. She knows that she has not chosen Michael, but God has ordained their relationship from the beginning of time. She knows that though she has been faithful in the work that God has given her to do to this point, there is a greater work that she and Michael must complete together. She is determined to allow God to be glorified in everything that she does and she knows that He will provide everything she needs. As Victoria and Michael honored God in their friendship and engagement, He will continue to be honored in their marriage. She knows the younger girls in her church look up to her. She will contin-ue to teach them how to live as a virtuous woman and to show them how God will reward them for their obedience to His will for their lives. As she lived a full and complete life as a single, she looks forward to living an abundant life in marriage.

We will never be happy in our career, marriage, or anything else, until we learn to love ourselves. In order to love ourselves we have to begin to see ourselves through God's eyes. Once we begin to understand how great His purpose and plan is for our lives, we will want to live each day to the fullest. When we are operating in our God-given purpose, we will not only experience fulfillment and joy in our own lives, but the lives of others will be changed around us. Our family, friends, and community will be blessed by the gifts God has placed within us. They are gifts that are meant to be shared with others. You will bring God glory as you walk in His light. When we seek Him first and His righteousness, everything we need will be given to us. We never have to worry about provision for a God-given vision. If He has called us to it, it is His responsibility to bring us through it. He is truly the only ONE who gives us unconditional love and everything we need to live life abundantly.

Prayer

Lord, I thank you for the freedom you have given me in Christ Jesus. Regardless of the negative things that may have happened in my past, I know that you have already worked everything out for my good as I pursue your purpose for my life. I thank you for revealing the root of any destructive patterns in my life. No longer will people or anything else come before you in my life. I thank you for the new life I have in You. You are doing a new thing in me and I am excited to see it unfold. I pray that I live each day grateful for the blessings that I have in You. I know that the gifts you have placed within me are not just to bless my life, but to change the lives of everyone around me.

THE ONE

Questions for Small Groups

Small Group Discussion:
It is important that you receive accountability from other godly women. I encourage you to meet regularly with other women to go through key concepts found in the book. Each chapter is broken into weekly discussions. I pray you enjoy the interaction as you probe deeper in your weekly discussions. The weekly discussions are perfect for women's ministry groups, discipleship circles, book clubs, and simply girlfriends that want to discuss their challenges in singleness. Everyone does not have to be single in fact, single women can learn from married women in the group. Enjoy your discussions.

THE ONE

Week 1: Introduction

1. Which of the seven characters do you most relate to and what similarities do you share?

_____

_____

_____

_____

_____

2. Each of the characters had areas in which she needed to seek God's counsel. In what areas of your life do you need to seek God's direction or deliverance?

_____

_____

_____

_____

_____

3. What was your fantasy of the perfect wedding day?

_____

_____

_____

_____

_____

4. Do you sometimes feel pressured to be married?

_____

_____

_____

_____

_____

5. How do you feel about being single?

_____
_____
_____
_____
_____

6. What are the blessings that come with being single?

_____
_____
_____
_____
_____

7. What are some of the challenges you face in singleness?

_____
_____
_____
_____

Week 2: No Greater Love, Know Greater Love

1. Is there an area of your life where you have desired to take the lead role?

_____
_____
_____
_____

2. Is there a woman of God that can hold you accountable to trust God in what seems like an impossible situation?

_____

_____

_____

_____

3. Lonely Lauri cannot see past the pain and hurt of her previous relationship. Is there anyone you have not for given for hurting you in a past relationship?

_____

_____

_____

_____

_____

4. How can you begin to give your heart more completely to God?

_____

_____

_____

_____

_____

5. Busy Brittany is always on the go. Can you relate to her struggle to make time for God?

_____

_____

_____

_____

_____

6. How can you begin to make God more of a priority in your life?

_____

_____

_____

_____

_____

7. Desperate Debra, is willing to do whatever it takes to get what she wants. Have you found yourself manipulating situations or people to get your way?

_____

_____

_____

_____

Week 3: Our Provider

1. How can you plan to spend consistent time with God in order to seek His directions each day?

_____

_____

_____

_____

_____

2. Is there anything in your life that seemed good, but is now hindering you from attaining God's best for your life?

_____

_____

_____

_____

3. What are some areas in which you need God's provision?

_____
_____
_____
_____
_____

4. How can you walk in greater faith in these areas?

_____
_____
_____
_____
_____

5. List some scripture references that relate to God's provision for your life.

_____
_____
_____
_____
_____

6. How has God provided for you in these areas in the past?

_____
_____
_____
_____
_____

7. What did you learn as you went through these trials?

_____

_____

_____

_____

_____

Week 4: Presenting God Our Whole Heart

1. Is there anything keeping you from giving God your whole heart?

_____

_____

_____

_____

_____

2. Is there anyone you need to forgive so that your heart does not become hardened?

_____

_____

_____

_____

_____

3. Is there any area of your life, where your heart is not completely yielded to God?

_____

_____

_____

_____

_____

4. Do you find yourself carrying past pain into new relationships?

_____

_____

_____

_____

_____

5. Do you find yourself fearful in entering new relationships? If so, why?

_____

_____

_____

_____

_____

6. How has the perfect love of God carried you in the past?

_____

_____

_____

_____

_____

7. How can you begin to give your heart to God more fully?

_____

_____

_____

_____

_____

Week 5: Giving God Our Best

1. What are some of the areas God has given you to be a steward over?

_____

_____

_____

_____

_____

2. Are there any areas where you have not given God your best?

_____

_____

_____

_____

_____

_____

3. What can you begin doing to become a better steward of your health?

_____

_____

_____

_____

_____

4. What can you begin doing to become a better steward of your finances? Are you faithful in your tithes and giving?

_____

_____

_____

5. What can you begin doing to become a better steward of your relationships?

_____

_____

_____

_____

_____

_____

6. How can you give of your time and other resources?

_____

_____

_____

_____

_____

_____

7. Are there some areas where you need to cut back, in order to give God more in a particular area?

_____

_____

_____

_____

_____

_____

Week 6: Letting Go, Letting God

1. Do you often feel uncomfortable when you are not in control? Explain.

_____

_____

_____

2. What areas do you need to let go of and let God handle?

_____
_____
_____
_____
_____

3. How can you trust God in your relationships?

_____
_____
_____
_____
_____

4. Are there negative relationships or experiences you need to let go of in order to healed and whole in God?

_____
_____
_____
_____
_____

5. How can you trust God more in your professional goals?

_____
_____
_____
_____
_____

6. What are some things on your to-do-list that you need to place on God's to-do list?

_____

_____

_____

_____

_____

7. What steps can you begin taking to allow God to handle those areas you are surrendering to Him?

_____

_____

_____

_____

_____

Week 7: Fit For the King

1. Do you find it difficult to submit to God in particular areas?

_____

_____

_____

_____

_____

2. Do you find it difficult to submit to others in authority?

_____

_____

_____

_____

_____

3. Esther had to go through a purification process. Do you
feel that you need purification in your mind, heart, or
soul?

_____

_____

_____

_____

_____

4. Are there people on your job, in your family, or in
ministry that you have failed to honor?

_____

_____

_____

_____

_____

5. Are others blessed by being in your presence?

_____

_____

_____

_____

_____

6. What things can you do to share the favor God has
given you with others?

_____

_____

_____

_____

_____

7. How can you begin to show Godly love to others in
   how you treat them?

_____

_____

_____

_____

_____

Week Eight: Pursuing Passion: A Single Purpose

1. What is your passion?

_____

_____

_____

_____

_____

2. How can you begin to pursue your passion and give
   God glory through your gifts?

_____

_____

_____

_____

_____

3. Do you meet or collaborate with others who share your
   passion?

_____

_____

_____

_____

_____

4. What core values do you strive to uphold in your life?

_____
_____
_____
_____
_____

5. Hesitant Heather was always delaying her dreams.
   Have you put your passion on hold or delay? If so,
   how can you pick it up again?

_____
_____
_____
_____
_____

6. If failure were not an option, what would you passionately pursue?

_____
_____
_____
_____
_____

7. If you could write a mission statement about who you
   are and your main purpose, how would it read?

_____
_____
_____
_____
_____

Bibliography

Introduction
I Cor. 7:32-33
Jer. 29:11-13, emphasis mine
Rom. 5:17

Chapter 1
James 4:8
Ps. 139:17-18
Luke 10:41-42
John 10:10
Marianne Williamson, A Return to Love: Reflections on the Principles of A Course in Miracles
Jer. 1:5
Ps. 34:4
John 4:10
Deut. 6:4
Deut. 6:5
Matthew 5:9-12
I Sam. 16:22
Gen. 24:12-14

Chapter 2
Long, Eddie. Called to Conquer.2000. Thomas Nelson Publishers
Philippians 2:3
Philippians 2:5-9
Genesis 12:1-2
Ps. 37:25
Phil. 4:19
Mathew 19:29
Isaiah 55:8-9
Psalms 37:5
Prov. 31:11-25
Prov. 10:22
Prov. 31:28-30

Chapter 3
Ps. 37:7
Genesis 22:12, KJV
Mathew 26:39
Mark 5:34
Mathew 21:22
Proverbs 3:5-6
James 1:5
Ps. 8:3-4
Luke 1:34
Luke 1:38
Luke 1:37
T.D. Jakes, Holy Bible: Woman Thou Art Loosed Edition, p.1025
Isaiah 54:4-5
Genesis 3:6
James 1:16-17
James 1:2-4

Chapter 4
Psalm 119:2
Hebrews 4:7
Psalm 51: 10
I Corinthians 13:2
I Corinthians 13: 4-8a (The Message)
I Corinthians 4:6-7
Luke 1:45
Revelation 2:4
Ephesians 2:4-5
Ephesians 3:17-18
Ps. 139:5-6 (The Message Bible)
Ephesians 5:3

Chapter 5
II Cor. 9:6-7
Isaiah 55:8-11
Ruth 1:16-17 (The Message Bible)

THE ONE

Psalm 37:25
Malachi 3:10
Psalm 126:5
Galatians 6:7-9
Matt. 25:23

Chapter 6
Larry Eisenberg
Matthew 16:25
Luke 6: 38
Job 1:21
Job 1:22
Philippians 3: 13-14
Isaiah 43:18-19
Psalm 138:8
Matt. 6:33-34

Chapter 7
Eccl. 3:11
Esther 4:14
Psalm 100:4
Proverbs 18:22
Holy Bible Woman Thou Art Loosed Edition, p.701.
Psalm 40:1
Philippians 4:6-7
Amos 3:3

Chapter 8
Deut. 30:19 NLT

ABOUT THE AUTHOR
TONIA N. EAST

Tonia's life is a perpetually unfolding success story, thanks to 3 things: communication, passion and faith.

As a teenager she realized she loved to speak and her effectiveness as a communicator was a key to opening doors and achieving success. Her passion for speech communication fueled her pursuit of a dual B.A. degree in Speech Communication and Political Science from Pepperdine University. She originally thought she would be a lawyer, but God had other plans in mind. Tonia decided it was time to leave Southern California and went on to pursue a Master of Arts degree in Speech Communication from the University of Georgia. Currently, she is completing a Ph.D in Communication at Georgia State University. Tonia has taught Public Speaking, Business and Professional Communication, and Voice and Diction for various universities.

Today as the founder and CEO of Pala Communication and a professor of Speech Communication, she uses public speaking, classroom instruction and training to empower college students, entertainers, and professionals to reach their goals. Pala Communication has helped individuals who are leaders in business, media, and entertainment to improve their communication skills.

Tonia's first book, Changing Lanes: A New Adult's Guide to Understanding Your Lane in Life was completed in 2005. Introducing this book, which helps people answer the question, "What am I supposed to do with my life?" has been a blast.

Tonia would love to hear your questions or comments about THE ONE. She is also available to speak at group discussions, conferences, book groups, or other engagements by contacting her at the following address or at www.toniaspeaks.com.

Pala Communication
PO Box 92157
Atlanta, GA 30314
Email: info@palacommunication.com
www.palacommunication.com